MasterChef

The Masters at Home

MasterChef

The Masters at Home

Recipes, stories & photographs

Photographed by David Loftus

Absolute Press
An imprint of Bloomsbury Publishing Plc

50 Bedford Square   1385 Broadway
London   New York
WC1B 3DP   NY 10018
UK   USA

ABSOLUTE PRESS and the A. logo are trademarks of Bloomsbury Publishing Plc

First published 2015

British Library Cataloguing-in-Publication Data
A catalogue record for this book is available from the British Library.

Library of Congress Cataloguing-in-Publication data has been applied for.

ISBN: HB: 978-1-4729-0411-9
ePDF: 978-1-4729-2162-8
ePub: 978-1-4729-2163-5

2 4 6 8 10 11 9 7 5 3

Printed and bound in Barcelona, Spain by Tallers Gràfics Soler

To find out more about our authors and books visit www.bloomsbury.com.
Here you will find extracts, author interviews, details of forthcoming events and the option
to sign up for our newsletters.

Contents

10 Ferran **Adrià**

20 Andoni **Aduriz**

30 Michael **Anthony**

40 Elena **Arzak**

50 Jason **Atherton**

60 Joe **Bastianich**

70 Lidia **Bastianich**

80 Claude **Bosi**

90
Massimo **Bottura**

100
Claire **Clark**

110
Wylie **Dufresne**

120
Graham **Elliot**

130
Andrew **Fairlie**

140
Peter **Gilmore**

150
Peter **Gordon**

160
Bill **Granger**

170 Angela **Hartnett**

180 Tom **Kerridge**

190 Tom **Kitchin**

200 Atul **Kochhar**

210 Pierre **Koffmann**

220 Jamie **Oliver**

230 Ashley **Palmer-Watts**

240 Neil **Perry**

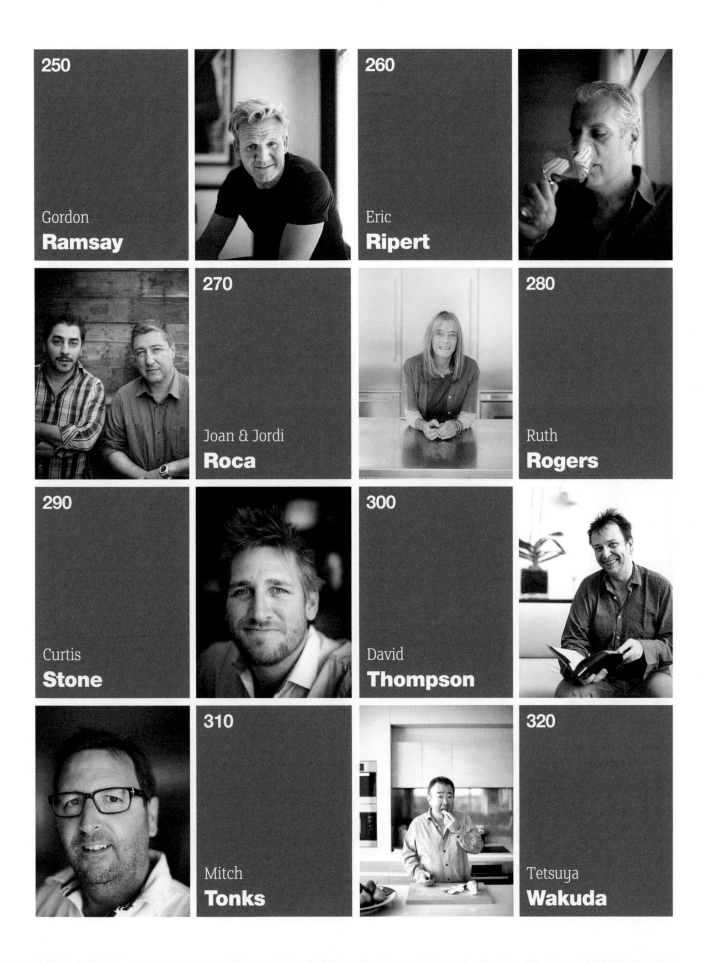

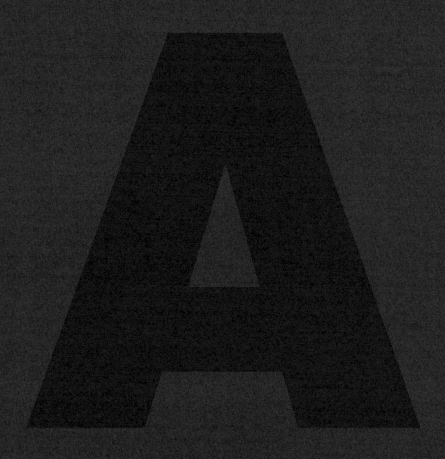

Ferran

Adrià

'One of my favourite food memories is of my mother's potato tortilla.'

Adrià

Widely considered to be one of the greatest chefs the world has ever known, Ferran Adrià is responsible for changing the face of modern gastronomy and inspiring a generation of boundary-pushing chefs through the cuisine at his famous restaurant, elBulli, in Roses on Spain's Costa Brava.

Adrià's food was the first to be dubbed 'molecular' in the late 1990s and it was he who pioneered the use of culinary foams, emulsifiers, gelling agents like xanthan and acidifiers for so-called 'spherification' (capturing flavour in little pearls that exploded in the mouth when eaten).

However, as a young man Adrià dreamed of a life as a footballer ('I wanted to be Johan Cruyff'). It was only a chance job washing dishes in a hotel to pay for a holiday in Ibiza that opened his eyes to the possibility of cooking for a career.

The chef at the hotel taught him traditional Spanish cooking and he went on to gain experience in a number of prestigious French kitchens before joining elBulli (then a traditional French restaurant) aged 22 as a line cook. Less than 18 months later he was head chef, eventually becoming chef-patron. The rest is history, with Adrià leading elBulli to many international honours, including three-Michelin-stars and being named as the best restaurant in the world in *Restaurant* magazine's annual San Pellegrino World's 50 Best Restaurants list five times.

Adrià closed elBulli in 2011, replacing it with his elBulli Foundation – dedicated to furthering gastronomic innovation – and elBulli 1846, a museum and visitor centre in Barcelona, themed around the restaurant and dishes he so famously created. There's also the Bullipedia project, an on-line encyclopaedia, and elBulli DNA, his laboratory in which he continues to seek new ways of looking at and interpreting fine-dining. 'elBulli never closed, it's simply being transformed.'

Yet despite his culinary trailblazing, Adrià is grounded in normality when he's off-duty. When he travels he always visits local markets, food shops and kitchenware stores ('it's a way of understanding the culture of a place'). Dinners at home are usually simple affairs involving vegetables, grilled fish and 'lots of fruit'.

Given half a chance, he'll opt for shellfish on the table and has to stop himself from over indulging on it. 'If I eat it five days running it's not funny!'

• • •

Secret Food Haunt

Amorino, a chic ice cream bar in Barcelona, near the elBulli Foundation workshop ('I'm secretly obsessed with ice cream'). It churns ice cream fresh every day, using carefully sourced produce including coconuts from Sri Lanka, Amalfi lemons and Ecuadorian chocolate. Launched in 2002 in France and Italy, the company now has outlets in cities all over the world, including London and New York.

Watermelon, Tomato and Basil Soup

*Refreshing and fun, you can serve this as
a main dish, a cocktail or in a tall glass.*

Serves 2

For the soup
3 large ripe tomatoes, or 800g ripe
   cherry tomatoes, finely diced
flesh from ¼ watermelon, seeded and
   finely diced (400–500g)
ground chilli pepper, cayenne pepper
   or Tabasco sauce, to taste
salt

For the basil oil
a small handful of basil with stalks
   attached
about 100ml extra virgin olive oil
salt

To garnish
6 cherry tomatoes
6 thin slices (2cm) of watermelon flesh

Pass the diced tomatoes and watermelon through a sieve into a bowl to obtain a smooth texture. Season to taste with salt and chilli pepper – or, if you prefer, cayenne or Tabasco sauce. Chill the soup.

To make the basil oil, remove most of the leaves from the basil stalks (keeping back a few leaves for garnishing) and put them in a blender with the olive oil and a little salt. Blend until smooth. Leave to infuse, then pass the oil through a sieve.

Blanch the cherry tomatoes for the garnish in boiling water for a few seconds. Remove them from the water and drop them into a bowl of cold water. Once cool enough to handle, peel off the skin.

To serve, divide the soup between two bowls. Garnish with the watermelon slices, cherry tomatoes, basil oil and reserved basil leaves.

• • •

Quail Legs with Soy

*This is an imaginative way of preparing quail – and with a little practice
they are a quick and surefire way of surprising your guests.*

Serves 2

4 quails
2 tablespoons plain flour
sunflower oil, for deep-frying
mixed green salad leaves

For the soy dressing
100ml light soy sauce
15g butter
1 teaspoon cornflour, mixed with a
   little water

First cut off the legs from the quails – pull a leg away from the carcass and cut through the loose skin, then free the leg (thigh and drumstick) by pulling against the joint to dislocate the thighbone. Using the tip of a sharp knife, bone out the thigh by cutting the flesh around the bone, keeping it within the skin. Leave the bone attached to the drumstick. Trim around the base of each drumstick, then push the meat up the bone so the drumstick looks a little like a lollipop.

Dust the legs with flour, then deep-fry them in the oil, heated to 180°C, for about 5 minutes or until golden. Remove and drain on kitchen paper. Keep hot.

Heat the soy sauce with the butter in a small saucepan and bring to the boil. Add the cornflour and stir until thickened.

Place some salad leaves in the centre of each bowl or one large serving bowl. Toss the legs in the soy dressing to coat, then add to the salad and serve.

. . .

Gratin of Red Fruits

*This is a dessert that combines the texture and taste of
crema Catalana with the freshness of yoghurt and red fruits.
You can include any fruit you like.*

Serves 2

3–4 heaped tablespoons mixed soft
   fruits (strawberries, raspberries,
   redcurrants and blackberries)
50g Greek yoghurt
chopped mint
40ml whipping cream, whipped until
   thick
caster sugar, to taste

For the crema Catalana
3 egg yolks
50g vanilla sugar, plus 2 extra
   tablespoons, for caramelising
1 heaped tablespoon cornflour
200ml milk

For the crema Catalana: place the egg yolks in a bowl with the sugar and whisk until they are creamy and reach the 'ribbon stage'. Whisk in the cornflour until the mixture is smooth. Scald the milk (but do not boil), then pour it into the egg and sugar mixture, whisking lightly until it is fully incorporated. Transfer the mixture to a clean saucepan and cook until thickened, stirring to prevent the custard getting lumpy. Once it is thick (but you can still pour it) take it off the heat and cool at room temperature.

Preheat the grill to high. Sprinkle the fruit over the bottom of two flameproof shallow serving bowls or into shallow dishes. Dab the yoghurt among the fruit.

Add a little chopped mint to the crema Catalana base, then fold in the whipped cream. Spoon this custard mixture over the fruit and spread it out to cover the fruit in a smooth layer. Sprinkle a fine layer of sugar on top.

Place under the grill to caramelise the sugar or, if you have one, use a kitchen blowtorch. Leave to set briefly before serving.

• • •

Andoni
Aduriz

'Olive oil, Idiazabal cheese and lots of wine are always in the larder.'

Aduriz

Andoni Luis Aduriz is one of Spain's most celebrated chefs, with dedicated fans as far afield as Japan, the USA and Latin America. A chef who plays with aroma, texture and flavour in a challenging, witty way at his two-Michelin-star restaurant Mugaritz in Spain's Basque country, he's a protégé of the great Ferran Adrià, but his own cooking lies somewhere between Adria's molecular alchemy and the ultra seasonal cooking of France's renowned Michel Bras.

After a less than glorious school record, it was Aduriz's mother who encouraged him to try culinary college in San Sebastián. After a sticky start (he had to retake the first year) he was infused with a passion for food, aged 16, and after graduating went on to work in some of Spain's top restaurants, eventually finding his way to Adrià's famous elBulli restaurant. 'He taught me to think originally and believe in myself.'

Weekends are hectic at Mugaritz, so Aduriz almost never has one free. But when he relaxes at home with his wife and son, he makes sure there are a few essentials in his larder. Olive oil, some local Basque Idiazabal cheese, 'lots of wine' and aerosol canisters of churros batter. 'I confess they're a weakness!'

Should friends drop round for dinner, 'a fiesta' of sardines would probably be on the barbecue and mackerel sashimi on the table, alongside seasonal ingredients. But between prolific book writing, a commitment to furthering culinary education at home and abroad and supporting several charities, Aduriz rarely has time to spare.

One thing he always has time to remember, though, is the debt he owes his mother, who not only set him on his career path, but also inspired him with her own cooking. 'The majority of my popular repertoire of recipes are inherited from her.'

• • •

Secret Food Haunt
La Bretxa market in San Sebastián, north-eastern Spain. A traditional, vibrant market – often used by the city's top chefs – selling fresh, local, seasonal produce including fruit and vegetables, meat, daily caught fish and charcuterie.

Leeks in Sesame Vinaigrette

Leeks in vinaigrette is an easy and popular recipe. My suggestion is to accompany them with a distinctive vinaigrette based on tahini or sesame paste. Obviously it's possible to replace the sesame seeds with hazelnuts, almonds or similar nuts that may be to hand.

Serves 4

3 leeks
3 fresh green garlic cloves
120g sesame seeds
4 tablespoons extra virgin olive oil
2 tablespoons sherry vinegar
2 tablespoons toasted sesame oil
   (optional)
salt

Wash the leeks, taking care to remove any soil from the green tops. Chop into 6–8cm pieces. Cook in a pan of boiling salted water for 10–15 minutes until they feel tender. Drain, then drop them into iced water to stop them cooking any further. Set aside.

Trim the garlic cloves and slice finely on the slant, including the stems. Reserve.

Roast the sesame seeds, in either a pan or a moderate oven, taking care to prevent them from burning. Put them in a food processor with 1 tablespoon water and blitz to a paste that is neither too thick nor too light. (You can also do this with a mortar and pestle, adding the water drop by drop).

Transfer the sesame paste to a bowl and mix in the olive oil, vinegar, some salt and the optional sesame oil. I prefer this dressing to be separated rather than emulsified.

To serve, warm the leeks in the oven preheated to 100°C (conventional oven 120°C/Gas Mark ½), then coat them with the sauce. Pile them in a bowl or on a serving dish and sprinkle the sliced garlic over them.

● ● ●

Wing Rib of Beef Sautéed with Herbs, Radish and Spring Onion

It is common to find 'txuleta' with garnishes such as roasted peppers and potatoes. In this special recipe, the mixture of aromatic herbs and crunchy vegetables brings with it freshness and a clash of textures. A delicious bite.

Serves 4

a small bunch of parsley
a handful of basil leaves
1 x 1.25kg beef wing rib joint (wing ribs are the first three ribs at the tender loin end of beef)
a small bunch of chives, cut into 2–3cm lengths
2 spring onions, finely shredded
2 radishes, thinly sliced
2 tablespoons extra virgin olive oil
salt

Wash and dry the parsley and basil, then pick off the small leaves and reserve these for the garnish.

You can prepare the beef yourself or ask your butcher to do it for you. Remove the eye muscle (think sirloin steak), with a little of the flank, from the bone. Cut into six pieces. Divide the bone itself, with any meat and fat still attached, into four pieces.

Heat a sauté pan and put in the pieces of bone. When the fat on the bone has rendered some of its dripping, add the pieces of beef and sear on both sides, then cook them according to your preference. Personally I like my steak rare.

Season the beef with salt and leave to rest for 3–4 minutes. Dress on serving plates with the picked herb leaves, chives, spring onions, radishes and olive oil.

● ● ●

Caramelised French Toast Empanada

This dessert traditionally takes advantage of unwanted pieces to create a sublime bite. The French toast, juicy and hot, contrasts with and perfectly complements the sheep's milk ice cream.

Serves 12

1 x 400g brioche or panettone
unsalted butter, for frying
caster sugar, for sprinkling and
    caramelising
sheep's milk ice cream, to serve

For the candied lemon peel
thinly pared peel of ½ lemon
200g caster sugar

For the pastry cream
125ml milk
12g cornflour
30g caster sugar
30g egg yolks
12g unsalted butter, cut into small
    cubes

For the almond cream
125g unsalted butter, at room
    temperature
1 egg and 1 egg yolk
150g pastry cream (see above)
125g ground almonds
1 tablespoon dark rum

To soak the 'French toast'
3 eggs
100g caster sugar
500ml milk
500ml whipping cream

A few days before serving, make the candied peel. Slice the lemon peel into matchsticks, then blanch for 2 seconds in boiling water and drain. Repeat the blanching three times. Make a syrup by dissolving the sugar in 200ml water and bringing to the boil. Pour into a bowl. Add the lemon peel and leave to soak in the syrup.

To make the pastry cream, heat 100ml of the milk in a heavy-based pan until boiling. In a bowl combine the rest of the milk with the cornflour and sugar to make a paste. When the milk in the pan is boiling, pour it into the bowl, stirring well to mix with the paste. Return to the pan and bring back to the boil, stirring, then simmer for 15 minutes to make a thick custard, stirring occasionally.

Beat the egg yolk with a little of the custard in a bowl. Whisk this into the rest of the custard in the pan, then remove from the heat. Cool until the temperature of the mixture is 60°C before beating in the butter a few cubes at a time. Set aside.

For the almond cream, beat the butter until creamy, then mix with the other ingredients until thoroughly amalgamated. Spread the almond cream on to a sheet of baking parchment and cover with clingfilm to prevent a skin from forming. Leave to set.

Now prepare the mixture for soaking the French toast. Mix the eggs with the sugar in a shallow dish, stirring until the sugar has dissolved, then add the milk and cream.

Cut the brioche into 12 slices, each weighing about 60g. Lay them, side by side, in the prepared soaking mixture and leave in a cool place or the fridge for 2 hours.

Heat some butter with a sprinkling of sugar in a non-stick frying pan, taking care not to burn the sugar. Very carefully lift the soaked brioche slices out of the dish and gently lay them in the pan. Fry until nicely coloured on both sides. Remove from the pan and set aside on a baking sheet.

When ready to serve, reheat the French toast in a hot oven for a few minutes. Meanwhile, cut out shapes from the set almond cream to fit the toast. Lay an almond cream shape on top of each piece of toast. Dust with sugar and caramelise with a kitchen blowtorch or for a few moments under a very hot grill. Serve immediately, with a scoop of ice cream and the candied lemon peel.

• • •

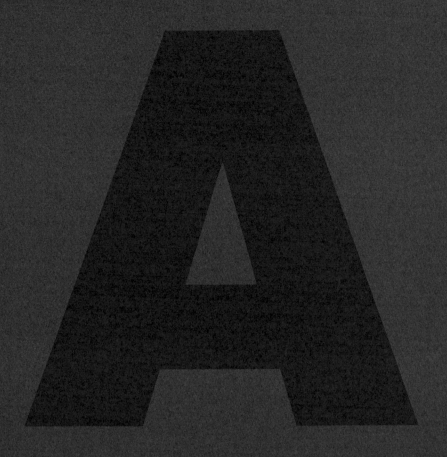

Michael
Anthony

'My favourite season is fall. It's filled with abundance.'

Anthony

It was, remarkably, in Japan where Cincinnati-raised Michael Anthony was first inspired to cook the French cuisine that he has become synonymous with at New York's famous Gramercy Tavern.

Inspired by the vibrant food scene in Tokyo, where he went as a degree student to hone his language skills, Anthony started work at a French restaurant, Bistro Shima, under Japan's quirky female chef Shizuyo Shima, who taught him classic French cooking techniques. At her insistence, he enrolled in Paris' Grégoire Ferrandi culinary school in 1992, graduating straight into the revered kitchens of Parisian giants Alain Passard at Arpège and Pascal Barbot at Astrance.

His kitchen skills honed, Anthony returned to the USA, and to New York, working first with renowned French chef Daniel Boulud but really making a name for himself at West Village's Blue Hill restaurant. Here he was spotted by New York's chef-restaurateur par excellence, Danny Meyer, who invited him to take over the kitchen at his legendary Gramercy Tavern.

The Gramercy's elegant no-airs-and-graces brasserie style of cuisine proved a natural fit for Anthony. Cooking here, he was able to reference both the rich layers of his French training and his American culinary heritage. Under his leadership the restaurant earned a three-star *New York Times* review and two James Beard awards, for Outstanding Restaurant and Outstanding Chef in New York.

At ease with modest ingredients, Anthony likes to champion vegetables, often centring on everyday staples – like the humble onion – in his dishes. Eggplant (aubergine) is his 'all-time favourite' vegetable – grilled, braised, fried or pickled.

Some chefs leave their uniform at work, but not Anthony. He cooks frequently for his wife and three daughters at home ('the chef's whites don't necessarily give me a free pass – they are very discerning!'), always in a clean kitchen ('really important'), often with family around and sometimes with a couple of glasses of wine standing by to set the mood.

Guilty pleasures include the odd tub of Häagen Dazs ice cream, while chocolate chip pancakes are a family favourite. There's also a regular spot for his mother's traditional Pennsylvanian Dutch 'pot pie' dish: 'basically vegetable soup with potato dumplings'.

• • •

Secret Food Haunt
Norwich Meadows Farm, in Chenango County, New York State, is an organic producer of vegetables, poultry and eggs that has an 'astounding variety' of fresh produce.

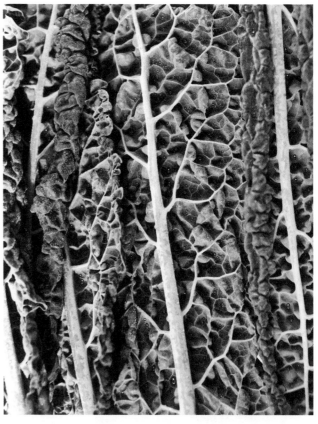

Kale and Ancient Grains Salad

Ancient grains are of interest to us because the story of these foods defines the beginning of civilisation. In pre-industrial times, grains represented a wide variety of flavours and textures. The plants themselves grew tall and became what's called a 'biomass', which produced many useable products as well as natural fertilisation of the soil. This dish really focuses on contemporary efforts to eat in a more delicious and sensible way, using a variety of grains to replace proteins and tell the story of local food heroes.

Serves 4

85g red quinoa
vegetable stock or water (see recipe)
95g farro
5 Jerusalem artichokes (about 150g
  in total), scrubbed
300ml olive oil
40g pitted dried dates, chopped
juice of ½ lemon
250g bunch of cavolo nero (black kale),
  ribs removed and leaves cut into
  2.5cm squares
120g assorted salad greens, such as
  baby mesclun
60g Sbrinz or other hard Swiss cheese
  such as cave-aged Gruyère, grated
45g flaked almonds, toasted
35g sunflower seeds, toasted

For the sorghum vinaigrette

20g sorghum syrup (you can substitute
  maple syrup)
2 teaspoons white balsamic vinegar
1 tablespoon lemon juice
1 teaspoon wholegrain mustard
185ml olive oil
salt and freshly ground black pepper

Preheat the oven to 180°C (conventional oven 200°C/Gas Mark 6).

Put the quinoa in a small saucepan with 500ml vegetable stock or water. Set over a medium heat and bring to the boil, then simmer for about 15 minutes until tender. Drain and allow to cool.

Combine the farro and 1 litre vegetable stock or water in another saucepan and simmer for about 25 minutes until tender. Drain and cool.

While the quinoa and farro are cooking, toss four of the whole Jerusalem artichokes with 2 tablespoons of the olive oil and a pinch of salt. Place on a baking tray and roast in the heated oven for about 30 minutes until tender. Leave to cool, then cut into bite-sized pieces.

Slice the remaining artichoke into thin coins, using a mandoline. Heat 240ml of the olive oil in a sauté pan over a medium–high–heat until the oil reaches 180°C. Carefully place the artichoke coins in the oil and fry, stirring frequently, until golden brown. Remove from the oil and drain on kitchen paper. Season with a pinch of salt.

To make the vinaigrette, mix together the sorghum syrup, vinegar, lemon juice and mustard in a bowl. Slowly stream in the olive oil while whisking until emulsified. Season to taste with salt and pepper.

In a mixing bowl, combine the cooked quinoa and farro with the chopped dates, roasted artichoke pieces, remaining 2 tablespoons olive oil, a squeeze of lemon juice and a pinch of salt. Divide among four shallow salad bowls.

Put the cavolo nero and salad greens in a large mixing bowl and dress to taste with sorghum vinaigrette. Divide among the salad bowls, on top of the grains. Top with the grated cheese, almonds, sunflower seeds and artichoke chips.

• • •

Raw and Roasted Root Vegetables with Black Bean Sauce, Herbed Ricotta and Anchovy Garlic Sauce

This dish was created when my then three-year-old daughter came to eat at Gramercy Tavern. I thought that we needed something colourful to keep her attention. This seasonal collection of vegetables, cooked and raw, with dipping sauces seems to keep more than just my child fixated.

Serves 4

7 medium heirloom carrots, in a variety of colours, scrubbed
6 medium parsnips, scrubbed
7 Jerusalem artichokes, scrubbed
2 tablespoons olive oil
6 globe radishes
grapeseed or groundnut oil, for deep-frying
15g butter
4 baby turnips, scrubbed and each cut into quarters

For the black bean dipping sauce
½ medium onion, cut into medium dice
1 small carrot, cut in half
2 tablespoons olive oil
1 garlic clove, thinly sliced
1 teaspoon very finely chopped jalapeño chilli
130g dried black beans, soaked overnight
white balsamic vinegar
salt

For the herbed ricotta
250g ricotta
4 tablespoons olive oil
grated zest and juice of 1 lemon
1 teaspoon very finely chopped parsley leaves
1 teaspoon very finely chopped dill
1 teaspoon very finely chopped tarragon leaves

For the anchovy garlic sauce
5 anchovy fillets, trimmed
2 egg yolks
260ml vegetable oil
½ garlic clove, finely grated
lemon juice
salt and freshly ground black pepper

Make the accompanying dipping sauces first. For the black bean sauce, sauté the onion and carrot in 1 tablespoon olive oil in a medium saucepan over a medium heat for about 5 minutes until lightly browned. Add the garlic and half of the jalapeño chilli, and sauté for a further 2–3 minutes just until cooked through. Add the drained beans, cover with water (about twice as much liquid as beans) and simmer over a medium heat for 45–50 minutes until the beans are fully cooked and very soft.

Remove from the heat and season with salt. Cool slightly, then remove and discard the carrot. Drain the beans, reserving the cooking liquid. Tip the beans into a blender and add the remaining chilli. Blend until smooth, adding enough of the reserved cooking liquid to keep the blade spinning loosely (no more than 240ml of liquid). Blend in the remaining olive oil. Season with additional salt and white balsamic vinegar to taste. The sauce should have a pourable consistency when cold. Cover and keep in the fridge until ready to serve.

To make the herbed ricotta, whisk the ricotta in a bowl and slowly drizzle in the olive oil until smooth. Fold in the lemon zest and herbs. Season to taste with a bit of lemon juice and salt. Keep in the fridge.

For the anchovy garlic sauce, finely chop the anchovy fillets into a paste. Put the egg yolks in a medium bowl and whisk to mix them together, then slowly stream in the vegetable oil while whisking until emulsified. Fold in the anchovy paste and garlic. Season to taste with lemon juice, salt and pepper. Keep in the fridge.

Preheat the oven to 180°C (conventional oven 200°C/Gas Mark 6).

Toss six of the carrots, four of the parsnips and six of the Jerusalem artichokes in a bowl with the olive oil, salt and pepper. Spread out on a baking tray lined with baking parchment and roast in the heated oven for 15 minutes until just tender. Remove from oven and cool, then cut into bite-sized pieces. Set aside.

Cut five of the radishes into quarters. Thinly shave the whole radish and the remaining raw carrot and artichoke; set aside.

Heat the vegetable oil in a deep-fat fryer or deep pan to 180°C. Using a mandoline, thinly slice the remaining two parsnips lengthways to about 3mm thickness. Deep-fry the parsnip slices for about 3 minutes until golden and crisp. Drain on kitchen paper and season with salt and pepper.

In a small sauté pan over a medium heat, sauté the roasted and cut pieces of artichoke and the roasted carrot and parsnip in the butter for about 5 minutes until nicely browned.

To serve, arrange the pieces of roasted and fried vegetables and the quartered raw radishes and turnips on a platter, or divide among plates. Garnish with the thinly shaved raw vegetables. Serve with the three sauces in bowls for dipping.

• • •

Roasted Asparagus
and Spiced Nuts

When asparagus finally arrives, it is a celebration here. The spiced nuts,
based on dukkah, and sweet and sour sherry glaze make these roasted
spears explode with flavour.

Serves 4

400g asparagus
2 tablespoons olive oil
85g honey
2 tablespoons sherry vinegar
35g pitted black olives, sliced (we use
    Taggiasca olives)
60g semi-soft, aged goat's cheese (we
    use Cremont from Vermont Butter &
    Cheese Creamery)
salt

For the spiced nuts
3g cumin seeds
2g black peppercorns
3g white sesame seeds
3g black sesame seeds
5g shelled unsalted pistachios
4g blanched almonds

For the braised pistachios
30g shelled unsalted pistachios
250ml olive oil
salt

First make the dukkah. Toast the seeds and spices, separately, in a small dry pan until they smell fragrant. Lightly crush the cumin seeds in a mortar and pestle; tip into a mixing bowl and reserve. In the same mortar, grind the black peppercorns with the pestle to a fine powder; add to the bowl. Then pound all the sesame seeds in the mortar to release their oils; add to the bowl.

Toast the pistachios and almonds in the dry pan over a medium heat for about 2 minutes until golden and fragrant, being careful not to burn them. Chop the nuts, then add to the dukkah along with salt to taste. Mix well. Store in a closed container in a dry place (the spiced nuts can be kept for up to a week).

For the braised pistachios, toast the nuts in a medium saucepan until fragrant. Add the olive oil and 1 teaspoon salt, reduce the heat to low and cook gently for 10–15 minutes until the pistachios are slightly soft. Remove from the heat and reserve the pistachios in the oil until ready to use.

Preheat the oven to 180°C (conventional oven 200°C/Gas Mark 6).

Snap the tough ends off the asparagus stalks. Reserve one of the asparagus spears, then season the rest with the olive oil and 2 teaspoons salt. Spread out on a baking sheet and roast in the heated oven for 15 minutes until fork tender. Leave to cool, then cut the spears lengthways in half. Set aside.

When ready to serve, place the asparagus in a large sauté pan over medium–high heat. Carefully add the honey and sherry vinegar to the pan and use a spoon or pastry brush to coat the asparagus with the vinegar and honey mixture. When the asparagus is hot, sprinkle the spiced nuts over the spears.

Divide the warm asparagus among four plates. Garnish with black olives, braised pistachios (drained of oil) and dollops of goat's cheese. Finish with pieces of shaved raw asparagus.

• • •

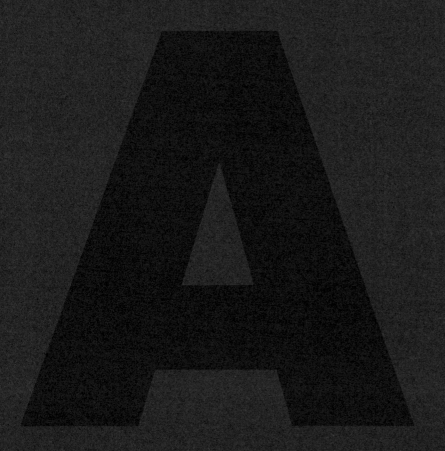

Elena
Arzak

'I like to have noise and action around me in the kitchen.'

Arzak

Spain's Elena Arzak may be famous for her ultra modern cuisine, dreamed up in a state-of-the-art development kitchen, but she's partial to doing a trail of pintxo (Basque tapas) bars in her home city of San Sebastián. And, indeed, she showcases traditional Basque ingredients in her own dishes, abiding by the mantra 'Basque, research, evolution, vanguard', when she dreams up new dishes.

Famous for dishes like 'the squid circle' – centred on cooked and tartare squid infused with orange peel, sarsaparilla and ginger – Arzak is rightly celebrated as one of the world's best female chefs. For well over a decade she's helped her equally famous father, Juan-Mari, retain the ultimate European cooking honour of three-Michelin-stars at the family restaurant in San Sebastián, north-eastern Spain. In 2014 they were awarded a Michelin star for their new London restaurant, Ametsa with Arzak Instruction, where Elena and her father regularly cook.

The fourth generation of her family to work at the restaurant, which was opened by the Arzaks over 100 years ago, Arzak worked two hours a day during her summer holidays in its kitchen from the age of 11 ('it was fun, not a job!'). Then, when she was older, she broadened her culinary training under iconic chefs in both France and England; and also at Ferran Adrià's ground-breaking elBulli in Spain.

Having grown up in a food-centric world, it's no surprise that she has now taught her own two children to cook. Not, yet, the challenging dishes of her restaurant, but less sophisticated fare. Anything with eggs, for instance: 'scrambled with fresh garlic, poached with potatoes or truffles, or as a chocolate omelette.' Or perhaps a dish her own mother passed down to her – porrusalda, a Basque soup made with leeks, potatoes and carrots.

Fish, as you'd expect in a Spanish family, is often on her home table. Cucumber and celery, though, are not ('I don't like them'). However, whatever dish is cooked a sieve is an integral part of the preparation process. 'I strain sauces, pasta, flour, sugar. For me it is essential.'

And also essential for Arzak – her 'guilty pleasure' – are percebes (goose barnacles), a traditional delicacy of the Basque country: 'I can eat lots of them!'

· · ·

Secret Food Haunt
Don Serapio, San Sebastián in north-east Spain. Located in Avenido Sancho el Sabio this food emporium-come-delicatessen specialises in local Basque produce and has an impressive selection of charcuterie, including Spain's famous jamon ham. Fresh fruit and vegetables, wines and cheese are also sold.

Clams in Squid Ink

*The clams are cooked lightly in the microwave so they retain their texture,
juices and flavour. They are accompanied by a rich, dark sauce called
'mojo negro', which originated in the Canaries.*

Serves 4

12 fresh, good-sized clams, cleaned as
   necessary

For the cereal powder
5g buckwheat (wholegrain)
5g barley (wholegrain)
5g millet (wholegrain)
5g rye (wholegrain)
olive oil, for frying

For the "mojo negro"
12g diced onion, fried until browned
10g diced green peppers, fried until
   tender and browned
5g toasted bread
½ garlic clove, chopped and fried until
   golden
10g baby squid ink sauce (from a
   sachet)
50ml water
7g black sesame seeds
1 teaspoon extra virgin olive oil
a squeeze of lemon juice

For the crumble
40g dried crustless bread
40ml extra virgin olive oil
50g fresh tomato juice
5g puréed red chillies (medium
   strength)
a pinch of caster sugar

For the confit potatoes
1 large potato (200g)
200ml smoked extra virgin olive oil

salt and freshly ground black pepper

The day before, make the cereal powder. Dry-roast each of the cereals separately
in a frying pan until toasted, then cook them in separate pans of boiling salted
water until tender. Drain and leave to dry completely overnight.

The next day, heat some olive oil and fry the different kinds of cereal until
they have puffed. Drain well on kitchen paper, then mix them together and
grind to a powder.

To make the "mojo negro", put all the ingredients in a blender and blend until
smooth. Season with salt and pepper. Set aside.

For the crumble, tear up the bread into tiny pieces and fry them in the olive
oil. Drain on kitchen paper and mix with the remaining crumble ingredients,
seasoning to taste with sugar, salt and pepper. Set aside.

Next, prepare the confit potatoes. Peel the potato and cut it into four even 3
x 1.5cm chunks. Put them in a pan, cover with the smoked oil and cook gently
until tender. This will take around 15 minutes. Drain and season with salt,
then keep warm.

Briefly cook the clams in the microwave, just until they can be opened using the
tip of a knife. Ensure that they remain whole.

To serve, put the clams on the potatoes and add the crumble and cereal
powder so that the different tastes and textures blend on the plate. Accompany
with the sauce.

Elena's tip
• Any leftover 'mojo negro' sauce can be kept in the fridge and used within 3 days.

• • •

Sea Bream with 'Mamia Rota'

This recipe has two ingredients that are very important in our Basque cuisine – fish and milk. Sheep's (ewe's) milk is used to make a soft curd cheese ('mamia rota'), which is served in a rich-flavoured broth with sea bream. Here in the Basque Country we are famous for our Idiazabal cheese, made from raw ewe's milk.

Serves 4

1 sea bream, about 400g, scaled and
    gutted/cleaned
olive oil, for poaching

For the smoked chicken broth
800g chicken pieces, with bone
1 tablespoon smoked extra virgin
    olive oil
xanthan gum
Lapsang Souchong tea leaves
salt and pepper

For the 'mamia rota'
200ml ewe's milk
10g sugar
1g salt
½ teaspoon liquid rennet (follow the
    instructions on the bottle for exact
    quantity)

For brining the fish
12g Lapsang Souchong tea leaves
1 litre boiling water
150g coarse salt
100ml extra virgin olive oil

For the garnish
fried, shelled pumpkin seeds
freeze-dried barley leaves

First make the smoked chicken broth. Preheat the oven to 170°C (conventional oven 190°C/Gas Mark 5). Rub the chicken with the oil and season it with salt and pepper. Place in a roasting tin and roast for 1 hour. Transfer the chicken to a large pot; set aside. Deglaze the roasting tin with a little water, stirring to mix in all the sediment, then reduce the liquid by half. Remove from the heat and reserve.

Cover the chicken with 2.5 litres water. Bring to the boil, then simmer for 4 hours, covered with a lid. Strain the broth and measure it, then thicken with xanthan gum, using 0.6g for every 250ml of broth. Add 2g Lapsang Souchong tea leaves for each 250ml of broth and infuse for 4 minutes. Stir in the reduced liquid from roasting the chicken, then strain the broth again. Set aside. (Keep the chicken for other uses).

For the 'mamia', stir the milk with the sugar and salt in a saucepan. Bring to boiling point, then cool to 37°C. Add the rennet, stirring, and leave the milk to curdle and form a junket. Once this has happened, keep in the fridge.

To prepare the brine, add the tea leaves to the boiling water and leave to infuse for 5 minutes, then strain into a bowl. Add the coarse salt and stir to dissolve. Allow the brine to cool.

Fillet the fish and cut it into 60g pieces. Make horizontal cuts 1cm deep in the skin. Add the fish to the tea brine and leave to marinate in the fridge for 2 hours.

Drain the pieces of fish and pat them dry. Put them in a clean bowl with the extra virgin olive oil and leave in the fridge for 12 hours.

When ready to serve, heat some olive oil to 56°C. Add the bream and poach in the oil for 7 minutes. Meanwhile, reheat the broth.

Ladle the broth into soup plates. Add the drained fish and pieces of curd ('mamia rota'), and garnish with pumpkin seeds and barley leaves.

. . .

Ugly Chocolate Tortilla

Eggs and chocolate have always worked together in many desserts but never before in this way! It doesn't look pretty – and we call it 'ugly' so everyone realises it's not supposed to have an attractive appearance – but it tastes wonderful!

Serves 4

For the passionfruit noodles
2 gelatine leaves
100g sieved passionfruit pulp
20g caster sugar

For the green lettuce sauce
1 large lettuce
125g caster sugar
10g honey
1 teaspoon cornflour, mixed with
   a little water

For the tortillas
2 eggs, beaten
50g caster sugar
50g dark chocolate (70% cocoa solids),
   chopped
scant 2 teaspoons cocoa powder

To serve
ice cream
edible pansies, to garnish

To make the passionfruit noodles, soak the gelatine in cold water until softened. Meanwhile, combine the passionfruit pulp and sugar in a small pan and bring to the boil, stirring to dissolve the sugar. Remove from the heat. Squeeze excess water from the gelatine, then add to the warm passionfruit mix and stir until melted. Pour on to a tray lined with a silicone sheet in a thin layer. Leave to cool and set before cutting into thickish strips.

To prepare the green lettuce sauce, purée the lettuce in a blender. Pour into a pan and add the sugar and honey. Simmer for a few minutes until the purée is softened. Thicken with the cornflour. Remove from the heat and leave to cool.

For the tortillas, mix together the ingredients in a bowl. Use half of the mixture to make each tortilla: fry in a lightly greased small pan over a medium heat, adding half of the passionfruit noodles to each tortilla. The tortillas should remain moist and juicy.

Turn out the tortillas on to a flat serving dish and roll up. Serve half a tortilla each with the lettuce sauce, some ice cream and a garnish of pansy petals.

• • •

Jason
Atherton

'Elegance and simplicity are what work for me.'

Atherton

Jason Atherton is one of the UK's most dynamic and switched-on restaurateurs. In little more than five years, since 2010, he went from owning no restaurants at all to heading up an international empire of 17 eateries (and he's still counting), stretching from London to Hong Kong, New York to Shanghai and Dubai to Singapore. He only cooks at one, though, his Michelin-star flagship restaurant Pollen Street Social, in London.

The wider public first became aware of Atherton as a result of his triumph on the BBC's popular television show, the Great British Menu, and though his rise to the top seems meteoric, in actuality there are 20 years of hard work in some of the toughest and most prestigious kitchens in Europe and England behind his current success.

Famously the first British chef to work in the kitchens of legendary Spanish restaurant elBulli, his entrepreneurial acumen was acquired over a decade of working for Gordon Ramsay, for whom he launched the popular and hugely successful Maze restaurant in London before leaving in 2010 to open Pollen Street Social.

With a large restaurant empire to run, Atherton has had to become adept at juggling business and family life. He is strict about his weekends, reserving them for his wife, Irha, and their two daughters, often cooking them the traditional Philippine dish of chicken and pork adobo.

The simplicity of his home cooking is a world away from the witty, clean flavoured food – fused from his knowledge of classical French and Asian cuisines, and the iconoclastic influence of elBulli – that Atherton cooks at work. It has more in common with his own modest beginnings in the British seaside town of Skegness, where his mother ran a guesthouse and his first brush with the stove was helping her do the breakfasts before going off to school.

In those days, as now, his mum made a 'great' apple pie: 'I often try to recreate it but it never tastes as good!' Baked beans on toast, on the other hand, always work.

However, one thing you can always count on in the Atherton household is a properly set table. Eldest daughter, Keziah, is responsible for this task. 'It's one thing I insist on. Cloth napkins, water and wine glasses and for late dinners a simple candle.'

• • •

Secret Food Haunt
Balham Farmers' Market in South London. Taking place every Saturday in Chestnut Grove School, close to Balham railway station, it hosts stalls for over 20 UK farmers and producers selling rare breed meat, poultry, dairy, bread, heritage fruit and vegetables and fish. It's also good for 'a spot of lunch'.

Cauliflower and
Crayfish Risotto

This is a risotto with a British twist featuring two fantastic local ingredients: cauliflower and crayfish. It is a Little Social recipe that our guests can't seem to get enough of. Here, a smooth cauliflower purée lightens the risotto and at the same time infuses it with a wonderful nutty flavour. The cauliflower acts as a base flavour for sweet, tender crayfish and creamy risotto rice. I think of this dish as a posh cousin of cauliflower cheese – comforting yet sophisticated.

Serves 4

For the cauliflower purée
1 head of cauliflower (about 300g)
300ml double cream
300ml whole milk
sea salt

For the crayfish bisque
1kg live crayfish, kept chilled
2 tablespoons olive oil
1 small onion, chopped
1 small carrot, chopped
2 garlic cloves, lightly crushed
1 lemongrass stalk, lightly bruised
3 white peppercorns
1 star anise
1 tablespoon tomato purée
80ml brandy
300ml dry white wine
600ml good-quality chicken stock
600ml good-quality veal or beef stock
3 sprigs of tarragon
3 sprigs of coriander
a handful of basil

For the risotto
200g risotto rice
200ml good-quality vegetable stock
25g grated Parmesan
25g mascarpone
40g unsalted butter

For the sautéed girolles
a knob of unsalted butter
1–2 tablespoons olive oil
200g girolles, cleaned
salt and pepper

For the sautéed cauliflower
50g unsalted butter
100g cauliflower, cut into tiny florets

Wash the crayfish, then put them into the freezer for about an hour to desensitise them and render them unconscious.

For the cauliflower purée, break the head into florets and set aside one large floret for garnish. Put the cream and milk in a saucepan and bring the mixture to the boil. Add the rest of the cauliflower and a generous pinch of salt. Simmer for 4–6 minutes until the cauliflower is soft. With a slotted spoon, transfer the cauliflower to a blender or food processor and blend to a smooth purée, adding a splash of the creamy milk if necessary (keep the leftover liquid in the pan to loosen the risotto if you need to). Pass the purée through a fine sieve into a saucepan. If making in advance, cover and chill once the purée has cooled.

For the crayfish bisque, bring a big pot of salted water to the boil. Have ready a large bowl of iced water. Parboil the crayfish in several batches, depending on the size of your pot. Keeping the water at a rolling boil, lower the crayfish into the pot and cook for 2 minutes. Remove the crayfish with a pair of tongs and immediately refresh them in the iced water. Once cool, extract the crayfish meat from the shells, keeping the shells to make the stock. Refrigerate the crayfish meat in a covered bowl until almost ready to serve.

To make the crayfish stock, heat the olive oil in a large pan placed over a medium–high heat. Tip in the onion, carrot, garlic, lemongrass, peppercorns and star anise. Sauté the vegetables, stirring frequently, until they are lightly browned. Add the tomato purée and stir over a high heat for a couple of minutes. Now add the crayfish shells, smash them with the base of a rolling pin to release more flavour and fry them for a minute. Add the brandy and white wine and boil until the liquid has reduced by half. Pour in the stocks and bring the liquid back to a simmer. Add the fresh herbs and simmer for 35–40 minutes until the bisque is flavourful. Pass the bisque through a fine sieve into a clean pan and return to the heat. Boil until reduced to a syrupy sauce consistency. Season to taste. Reheat the bisque before serving.

For the risotto, parboil the rice in a pan of salted water for 7 minutes. Drain well, then spread the rice out on a tray to cool quickly. When you are about ready to serve, bring the vegetable stock to the boil in a saucepan. Add the parboiled rice to the stock and simmer for 2 minutes to finish cooking. Add the cauliflower purée, followed by the grated Parmesan and mascarpone. Stir well, then taste and adjust the seasoning. Finally, add the butter to the risotto and stir until the rice is well coated and glossy. Take the pan off the heat and leave the risotto to stand for a few minutes while you fry the girolles and crayfish.

>

Heat the butter and oil in a wide frying pan over a medium–high heat. Add the girolles with a pinch of salt and pepper and fry for 3–5 minutes until any moisture released has cooked off. Add the crayfish meat to the pan and fry for another 2–3 minutes until the crayfish is just cooked through. Taste and adjust the seasoning. Take the pan off the heat.

To sauté the cauliflower, heat the butter in a frying pan, add the small cauliflower florets and some seasoning, and cook until the butter turns a nutty brown and the cauliflower is cooked through.

Divide the risotto among four warmed shallow bowls. Spoon a little bisque over the risotto, then top with the girolle and crayfish mixture and the sautéed cauliflower. To garnish, very thinly slice the reserved cauliflower floret (ideally using a mandoline) and scatter over each dish. Serve immediately.

• • •

Roast Venison and Beetroot
with Poached Pears

In the autumn, we always have this venison and beetroot dish on the menu at Pollen Street Social. Gamey venison has a natural affinity with sweet fruit, such as apples and pears, and it is wonderful with earthy beetroot.

Serves 6

6 x 100g boned loin of venison (ask your butcher for any trimmings for the sauce, if available)
25g unsalted butter
sea salt and freshly ground black pepper

For the roast beetroot
600g beetroots (a mixture of baby and normal-sized)
4 tablespoons caster sugar
4 sprigs of thyme
4 garlic cloves, peeled
4 teaspoons sea salt
a few dashes of sherry vinegar

For the spiced honey sauce
½ teaspoon lavender
½ teaspoon coriander seeds
½ teaspoon cumin seeds
¼ teaspoon Szechuan peppercorns
60ml sherry vinegar
25g unsalted butter
½ teaspoon sea salt
200ml clear honey
a squeeze of lemon juice

For the red wine sauce
1 tablespoon olive oil
1 shallot, sliced
1 garlic clove, chopped
1 sprig of thyme
¼ teaspoon white peppercorns
1 bay leaf
1 tablespoon sherry vinegar
325ml red wine
400ml good-quality veal or beef stock

For the spiced poached pears
375g caster sugar
1 tablespoon lemon juice
4–5 star anise, lightly crushed
4 cinnamon sticks
6 pears, peeled and cut into wedges

First, prepare the beetroots. Wash them and trim off the stalks. Place the baby and normal-sized roots into separate saucepans and cover with cold water. Add half the sugar, thyme, garlic, salt and a dash of vinegar to each pan. Simmer for 40–45 minutes until the beetroots are tender. Drain and leave to cool. When cool enough to handle, peel the beetroots and cut each one into 2.5cm cubes. Set aside.

For the spiced honey sauce, toast the lavender for a few seconds in a dry hot pan. Tip in the coriander seeds, cumin seeds and Szechuan peppercorns, and toast for a few more seconds until the spices release their oils and fragrance. Pour in the sherry vinegar and boil until it has reduced to a sticky glaze. Add the butter, salt and honey and bring back to a simmer. Continue to simmer until the sauce has reduced by two-thirds to a syrupy consistency. Strain it through a fine sieve and discard the spices. Season to taste with a little squeeze of lemon juice. Set aside until ready to serve.

Next, make the red wine sauce. Heat the oil in a heavy-based pan until hot. If you have them, add the venison trimmings and fry them over a medium–high heat until golden brown all over. Stir in the shallot and garlic and fry for a few minutes until they are lightly golden, then add the thyme, peppercorns and bay leaf. Deglaze the pan with the sherry vinegar and red wine, scraping the base of the pan with a wooden spoon to release any browned sediment. Boil the liquid until reduced by three-quarters. Add the stock and bring to the boil. Reduce the heat slightly and simmer for 20 minutes until the sauce is flavourful. Pass the sauce through a very fine sieve (or one lined with muslin) into a clean pan and boil steadily until reduced to a syrupy consistency. Set aside.

For the poached pears, put the sugar, lemon juice, spices and 1 litre water into a wide pan. Stir to dissolve the sugar, then bring the syrup to the boil. Gently lower the pears into the syrup. Cover the pears with a dampened piece of baking parchment roughly cut to the diameter of the pan. Simmer gently for 8–10 minutes until the pears are tender. Set aside.

To cook the venison, heat the butter over a medium heat in a heavy-based pan. Add the venison pieces and sear until golden brown all over, keeping the meat medium-rare. Cooking should take 5–8 minutes, depending on their thickness. Remove the venison to a warm tray and let the meat rest for a few minutes while you reheat the pears and sauces.

Place the beetroot pieces in a frying pan with 3 tablespoons of the spiced honey sauce and toss to coat. Heat for a couple of minutes, stirring frequently, until warmed through. Thickly slice the venison and divide among warmed plates. Serve with the spiced beetroot, poached pears and red wine sauce.

• • •

Chocolate Ganache with Spanish Olive Oil and Sugared Bread

Many of the tapas bars in Spain have a version of this modest dessert on their menu. It is simplicity at its best – just some really good chocolate ganache spread on lightly sweetened caramelised bread. A drizzle of good extra virgin olive oil and a tiny sprinkle of sea salt really bring the flavours alive.

Serves 4

100g dark chocolate (65–70% cocoa
  solids), roughly chopped
120ml double cream
a pinch of sea salt
extra virgin olive oil, preferably
  Spanish, for drizzling

For the sugared bread
4 slices of sourdough
softened unsalted butter, for spreading
icing sugar, for dusting

Place the chocolate in a bowl. Pour the double cream into a small saucepan and bring to the boil. As soon as it begins to bubble, tip it over the chocolate. Let it rest for 2 minutes, then whisk until the chocolate has melted and the mixture is smooth. Transfer the chocolate ganache to a clean jar or bowl and leave to cool.

Preheat the oven to 200°C (conventional oven 220°C/Gas Mark 7). Spread some butter on to both sides of the sourdough slices and dust each side with icing sugar. Arrange them in a single layer on a baking tray lined with baking parchment and toast in the oven for 8–10 minutes, turning once, until golden brown and crisp on both sides. Divide the sugared bread among individual serving plates then spread each one with the chocolate ganache. Drizzle with a little olive oil, add a sprinkle of sea salt and serve immediately.

• • •

Joe
Bastianich

'A meal without wine is called breakfast.'

Bastianich

ine expert, international restaurateur and television host, culinary show judge and reality show star: Joe Bastianich is all of the above and more, including triathlete, author and frustrated rock guitarist/song writer!

That he should have made a career in the restaurant world is no surprise. If ever there was somebody predestined to be a restaurateur it was Bastianich. Son of Lidia (one of the USA's most recognisable food broadcasters and restaurant owners) and Felice Bastianich, he grew up working in his parents much loved New York restaurant, first at Buonavia in Queens, and later at Felidia in Manhattan – starting off as a washer-upper and general kitchen hand – before carving his own career in the competitive New York City restaurant world, eventually expanding his empire with various business partners throughout the USA and overseas, including Singapore and Hong Kong.

However, it is Orsone, a bed & breakfast, restaurant and tavern opened with his mother Lidia, on the grounds of the Bastianich family winery in Friuli, Italy, that he considers to be on his dream site.

Among his many other businesses are the acclaimed and award-winning New York restaurant Babbo Ristorante e Enoteca, opened with chef Mario Batali in 1998, and the innovative Italian artisan superstore Eataly. This combines high-quality Italian produce outlets alongside restaurants and cafés under one roof and was co-launched in 2010 in the USA by Bastianich with his mother, Batali and Italian retail pioneer Oscar Farinetti.

Although not a chef by trade, Bastianich can grill a mean steak for family and friends, or cook authentic Italian dishes gleaned from his mother. 'I practically stole her jota [pronounced yoh-tah] recipe – an old farmhouse-style stew with pork and beans.' Lidia also taught him to always have

extra virgin olive oil in the store cupboard, 'of course!', but his love of singing and guitar playing is all his own. His most treasured possession is a Tobacco sunburst super jumbo guitar, which he plays in his band, The Ramps.

Bastianich's kitchen is always alive with 'the buzz of family' – his wife, Deanna, and their three children – and, naturally, when he's cooking there's music playing: 'something high energy. My favourites are Led Zeppelin, the Grateful Dead and the Foo Fighters!'

• • •

Secret Food Haunt
La Frasca, a restaurant in Lauzacco near Udine, in the Friuli region of north-east Italy. Owned by Valter Scarbolo, it showcases the local artisan produce and wine of the region. Home-made salumis are a speciality.

Tagliata with Rocket and Grana Padano

I travel a lot for MasterChef so I don't often have the time to cook, but when I do, either at home in Connecticut with the family, or over the summer when we spend a few months based in Italy, I like to cook this tagliata for dinner guests, served family-style. It's always a winner!

Serves 2

5 tablespoons extra virgin olive oil
1 garlic clove, finely chopped
1 x 350g piece of beef fillet or sirloin
 steak, about 4cm thick
1 teaspoon kosher or sea salt
1 teaspoon coarsely ground salt
1 teaspoon freshly ground black pepper
4 large handfuls of rocket
3 tablespoons balsamic vinegar
thick shavings of Grana Padano cheese

Heat 2 tablespoons of the olive oil in a cast-iron frying pan or ridged cast-iron grill pan over medium–high heat. Meanwhile, mix 1 tablespoon of olive oil with the garlic and rub over both sides of the steak. Season with the salt and pepper.

Lay the steak in the hot pan and sear for 3–4 minutes per side for rare, or 4–5 minutes per side for medium rare (it may need 1 more minute, depending on the thickness of the steak), moving the fillet as little as possible.

Remove the steak from the pan and leave to rest on a chopping board for 7–8 minutes before slicing against the grain into 1cm-thick pieces.

Divide the rocket among four plates and lightly dress with the remaining olive oil and the balsamic vinegar. Arrange four to five slices of steak on each plate and finish with shavings of cheese on the meat.

• • •

Rigatoni alla Norma

This is a recipe that everyone enjoys in my family. Eggplant (aubergine), tomatoes, ricotta… I mean, what's not to love? It's also a favourite on the menu at Becco, my first restaurant that I opened in 1993 in New York City.

Serves 4

4 tablespoons extra virgin olive oil, plus extra for drizzling
½ medium red onion, chopped into 5mm dice
4 garlic cloves, thickly sliced
2 medium aubergines, cut into 2.5cm cubes
2 x 400g cans of Italian plum tomatoes
2 sprigs of basil, plus leaves to garnish
1 sprig of thyme
red chilli flakes, to taste
450g rigatoni pasta
4 tablespoons soft ricotta cheese
a handful of chopped flat-leaf parsley leaves
salt and freshly ground black pepper

Heat the olive oil in a 30–35cm sauté pan until smoking. Add the onion and garlic and cook for 5–6 minutes until soft but not browned. Add the aubergines and cook, stirring regularly, for 8–10 minutes until softened and lightly browned. Add the tomatoes, basil and thyme sprigs and chilli flakes. Bring to the boil, then simmer for 15 minutes, stirring occasionally. Season to taste with salt and pepper and reduce the heat to very low so the sauce simmers gently.

Meanwhile, cook the pasta in a large pan of boiling salted water according to the packet directions, until al dente. Drain well, then pour the hot pasta into the pan with the aubergine mixture and mix together.

Top each serving with a dollop of ricotta and garnish with chopped parsley and basil leaves. Finish with a drizzle of olive oil.

Chicken Involtini

This simple recipe is one I came up with when I began training for marathons and needed something quick, easy and high in protein, but also low in cholesterol. Using frozen spinach in this dish is a more economical option for families, and can be time-saving as well. Keeping a stash of frozen veggies on hand is great for busy households that don't always have time for frequent trips to the grocery store or farmer's market.

Serves 4

4 large skinless, boneless chicken breasts
1 x 250–300g block of frozen leaf spinach, thawed
3 tablespoons Dijon mustard
4 tablespoons chicken stock
4 tablespoons olive oil
4 tablespoons white wine
about 70g dry breadcrumbs
a handful of chopped flat-leaf parsley
salt and freshly ground black pepper

Preheat the oven to 160°C (conventional oven 180°C/Gas Mark 4). Slice each chicken breast horizontally in half so you end up with eight thin pieces from the four breasts. Put them between sheets of greaseproof paper or clingfilm and pound to make them even thinner.

Cook the spinach in boiling water for several minutes. Drain well, pressing out excess liquid. Chop the spinach and mix with the Dijon mustard.

Spread the spinach over the top of the chicken pieces. Roll up each piece and secure with a wooden cocktail stick.

Place the chicken involtini in a baking dish, arranging them in one layer. Pour over the chicken stock, olive oil and white wine. Season with sea salt and freshly ground black pepper. Mix together the breadcrumbs and parsley and sprinkle evenly over the top. Bake for 30 minutes and serve hot.

• • •

Lidia
Bastianich

'I always have a centerpiece I make myself from flowers and greens from my garden.'

Bastianich

Lidia Bastianich's life is seared on to America's culinary history. As the head of one of the country's foremost restauranting families, she owns or part-owns more than ten eateries across the United States, including Felidia in New York and Lidia's in Kansas City. She's also an Emmy-award-winning television culinary broadcaster with her own production company, multi-cookbook writer and children's author. In 2010 in the USA, along with her son, Joe, she was a co-founder of the hugely successful Eataly, the global Italian artisanal superstore.

Born in Pula on the Adriatic (now in Croatia, but once part of Italy), Bastianich's parents emigrated to New York in 1958 when she was 11 years old. Thirteen years later, she opened her first restaurant with her husband and soon took the momentous decision to learn to be a chef on the job. She never looked back.

Both her restaurants and her home cooking, naturally, showcase authentic Italian cuisine – honest, simple, gutsy food. And it's not only Italian cooking that she references. Bastianich also likes to sip a 'well-made espresso', but with a little something to intensify the experience; the 'bittersweet' taste of high-quality chocolate and, possibly, 'a drop of Pyrat rum to rinse the coffee cup when done'.

Seafood is a 'hands down' family favourite, especially lobster risotto, perhaps preceded by a salmon or tuna tartare and followed by salad and grilled fish. The buzz of gathering all generations of her family around her while she cooks, from her 94-year-young mother to her grandchildren, is integral for Bastianich. 'I feel I not only transmit the knowledge of how to cook but also love and the meaning of sitting around a table with family and good food.'

Over the years, Bastianich has been showered with accolades for her restaurants, broadcasting and charity work, including two James Beard awards, the most prestigious hospitality awards in the USA. Despite this, she herself regards cooking for the former Roman Catholic pontiff Pope Benedict XVI, to be a pinnacle of her illustrious career.

Whether she confessed to the Pope her guilty pleasure of eating the odd peanut butter and grape jelly sandwich, only they know!

• • •

Secret Food Haunt
Farmer stands on the North Fork of Long Island, some 130-odd kilometres out of New York city. Farmers sell direct to the public: local, fresh, seasonal produce.

Raw and Cooked Salad

The 'insalate cruda/cotta' can vary to reflect the season. Here I use autumn and winter vegetables like squash and beetroot, but in the summer months you could cook green beans, zucchini (courgette) and others. With the addition of some tuna, sliced grilled chicken or cheese, this salad turns into a great main course.

Serves 6 or more

450g sweet onions (such as Supa-sweet, Vidalia or Walla Walla), cut into 2cm slices

120ml extra virgin olive oil, or as needed

225g peeled butternut or acorn squash, cut into 2.5cm cubes

300g beetroot

1–2 large, fresh ripe tomatoes (about 225g)

80g pitted black olives

3 tablespoons small capers, drained

3 tablespoons red wine vinegar

1–2 soft-leaf lettuces (about 350g), separated into leaves

coarse sea salt or kosher salt and freshly ground black pepper

Preheat the oven to 170°C (conventional oven 190°C/Gas Mark 5). For the 'verdura cotta' (cooked vegetables), brush the onion slices with some olive oil and sprinkle salt lightly on both sides. Lay the onions in one layer on a baking sheet and roast for about 20 minutes, turning once, until slightly softened and nicely caramelised on the flat sides and edges. Leave to cool, then separate the slices into thick onion rings.

Season the squash with a little salt and olive oil, then lay out on a baking tray lined with baking parchment and bake for 25 minutes until tender. Cool.

Cook the beetroot, skin on, in boiling water until tender (time depends on the size of the roots). Drain and cool, then peel and cut into slices.

For the 'verdura cruda' (raw vegetables), core the tomatoes, then slice them into wedges that are roughly the same size as the cooked vegetables.

Put everything in a large salad bowl except the lettuce: onions, squash, beetroot, tomatoes, olives and capers. Sprinkle with salt and freshly ground pepper and drizzle over the rest of the olive oil and the red wine vinegar. Tumble the vegetables to coat them with dressing. Scatter the lettuce on top, tearing the larger leaves in two, then toss the greens with the vegetables gently for about a minute, to distribute the dressing evenly. Taste and adjust the seasoning, and toss again.

Serve immediately – always giving each plate some of the heavier goodies that drop to the bottom of the bowl and hide under the lettuce.

● ● ●

Penne with Sausage, Onions and Fennel

An easy and delicious recipe, the ingredients are basic but the result is complex and truly satisfying. As these ingredients caramelise, layer upon layer of flavour will form. Italian sausage, onion, fennel bulb, crushed red pepper and tomato, a harmony of Italian products. Toss your pasta in this luscious sauce and finish off with a dusting of Grana Padano. This dish will become one of your family's favourites, as it is for our family.

Serves 6

450g sweet Italian sausages
1 large fennel bulb (about 450g)
3 tablespoons extra virgin olive oil
2 medium onions, cut into half-moon slices
½ teaspoon red chilli flakes
250ml crushed, or puréed and sieved, fresh San Marzano tomatoes (or good-quality plum tomatoes)
450g penne
4 tablespoons finely chopped parsley
100g pecorino or Grana Padano cheese, freshly grated
salt

Remove the sausage meat from its casing and break up the meat a bit with your fingers and set aside.

Trim the fennel bulb, removing any tough outer parts. Slice the bulb lengthways in half and remove the core, then cut each half lengthways into 5mm-thick slices. Separate the slivers of fennel if they are attached at the bottom; cut the long slivers in half so you have 5cm-long matchsticks of fennel.

Bring a large pot of salted water to the boil for the pasta. Meanwhile, heat the olive oil in a large frying pan over medium–high heat. Add the sausage meat and cook, stirring and breaking it up with a wooden spoon, for about 1½ minutes until it sizzles and begins to brown.

Push the sausage to the side of the pan and drop the onion slices into the cleared centre. Sauté, stirring, for about 2 minutes until the onions sizzle and wilt, then mix them into the sausage meat. Clear a new space and drop in the fennel. Leave it to heat up and wilt for 1 minute or more, then stir into the sausage mixture. Sprinkle in ½ teaspoon salt.

Clear a little spot in the pan and drop in the chilli flakes. Toast the flakes for 30 seconds, then stir to combine with the sausage mix. Plop in the tomato and stir it into the rest of the ingredients. Leave to simmer for 5 minutes or so while you cook the pasta.

Drop the penne into the boiling water, then bring back to the boil and cook until the penne are al dente. Drain, reserving about 240ml of the pasta water.

Pour the reserved pasta water into the frying pan and stir well, then bring back to the boil. Reduce to a simmer and cook for about 6 minutes until the flavours have developed, the sauce is thickened but not too thick, and the fennel is soft but not mushy. (Add more water if the sauce reduces too rapidly). Season to taste.

Drop the cooked penne into the simmering sauce and toss everything together until the pasta is coated with the sauce. Sprinkle with the chopped parsley.

Remove the pan from the heat. Sprinkle the grated cheese over the pasta and toss it to mix. Serve straight from the pan into warm pasta bowls.

• • •

Oven-braised Pork Chops
with Red Onions and Pears

I love cooked fruit with meats, especially the fattier meats and roasts. Here, in addition to the pears, the honey helps to caramelise the pork, onion and pears as they oven-braise. It is a technique that works well with other roasted meats and birds too. Just mix a little honey with the pan juices and baste or brush the roast with that during the last ten minutes or so of roasting.

Serves 4

500ml balsamic vinegar
3 tablespoons extra virgin olive oil
6 garlic cloves, peeled
8 medium-sized cipollini onions
(400–450g in total), cleaned
4 centre-cut pork rib chops 3cm thick,
each about 350g
4 bay leaves
2 ripe but firm Bosc pears, peeled,
cored and each cut into 8 wedges
4 tablespoons red wine vinegar
2 tablespoons clear honey
salt and freshly ground black pepper

In a small saucepan, bring the balsamic vinegar to the boil over a high heat. Adjust the heat to a gentle boil and boil until the vinegar is syrupy and reduced to about 80ml. Set aside.

Preheat the oven to 200°C (conventional oven 220°C/Gas Mark 7). Heat the oil in a large, heavy, ovenproof frying pan over medium–high heat. Whack the garlic cloves with the flat side of a knife, then scatter them in the oil and add the cipollini onions. Cook for about 5 minutes, shaking the pan frequently, until the onions are browned. Remove the garlic and cipollini onions from the pan and set aside.

Lay the pork chops in the hot pan and cook for about 6 minutes until the underside is browned. Turn the chops over and return the cipollini and garlic to the pan. Add the bay leaves. Cook for another 6 minutes until the second side of the chops is browned. About halfway through browning the second side, tuck the pear wedges in between the chops. Season with salt and pepper.

Stir the red wine vinegar and honey together in a small bowl until the honey is dissolved. Pour the vinegar/honey mixture into the frying pan and bring to a vigorous boil.

Transfer the pan to the oven and roast for about 30 minutes until the onions and pears are tender and the juices from the pork are a rich, syrupy dark brown. Once or twice during roasting, turn the chops and redistribute the onions and pears. Handle the pan carefully as it will be extremely hot.

Remove the pan from the oven. Place a chop in the centre of each warmed serving plate. Discard the bay leaves from the onion-pear mixture and check the seasoning, adding salt and pepper if necessary. Spoon the pears, onions and pan juices around the chops. Drizzle the balsamic vinegar reduction around the edge of the plate and serve.

• • •

Claude
Bosi

'How do I relax? Very easily!'

Bosi

I f ever a man was destined to be a chef, it was Claude Bosi. The scion of a restaurateuring family from Lyon, he had food surrounding him from the moment he was born. So it's no surprise that he's an internationally recognised Relais & Chateaux Grande Chef du Monde, or that he's ended up with two-Michelin-stars for his restaurant, Hibiscus. The only surprise is that Hibiscus is in London, not France.

The reason for this is that like many a French chef before him, Bosi travelled to the UK in 1997 to learn English, found the country suited him and never went back. He crossed the English Channel having worked in some of France's most legendary kitchens but started his English career modestly, as head chef of a country hotel in Ludlow, Shropshire for which he quickly won culinary recognition.

That success emboldened Bosi and his ex-wife Claire to open the first incarnation of Hibiscus in Ludlow in 2000. In three short years he achieved two-Michelin-stars for the restaurant but after seven years the bright lights of London tempted him to move Hibiscus to the capital, where it is to this day. (He retains a link with Ludlow through a hotel jointly owned with his brother Cederic, bought in 2014).

As a chef Bosi has never been afraid to blend his formidable French training with the culinary influences of the world around him, be they from Poland, Japan or, indeed, Britain. He's a great fan of English puddings – boozy trifle in particular – and won a legion of fans for his fine-dining take on the humble British sausage roll when he opened in London.

His cooking is complex, though less complicated than it was, with inspiring flavour combinations, but he's always led by the seasons and the British produce he showcases in his dishes.

On the whole, he cooks at home for wife, Lucy, and the rest of his friends and family as he does in his restaurant, making few concessions to being out of the professional kitchen, but a traditional roast chicken, with new potatoes and seasonal vegetables, always has a place on the Bosi family table. And no doubt there's a tin full of Mars Bars somewhere, too (out of the reach of daughter Paige and son Freddie), as snacking on the British chocolate covered sweet is his self-confessed guilty pleasure!

• • •

Secret Food Haunt
Madeleine Patisserie in Clapham, South London. Located off Clapham Common, everything is made on site in this French style café. It sells all the viennoiserie pastries you'd expect (Danish, croissants, pain au chocolat etc). Citron tarts and macarons are a speciality, as is rustic bread. Snacks like the traditional croque-monsieur are also sold.

Soused Mackerel, Rhubarb, Mushroom and Smoked Mackerel Purée

*Smoked mackerel is one of my favourite ways to eat mackerel, so
I make this a lot at home. The flavour of the Japanese ingredients
and the rhubarb cut through the richness of the fish and make a
very beautiful, delicate starter.*

Serves 4

For the soused mackerel
4 x 50g fresh mackerel fillets
200ml rice wine vinegar
5g Japanese kuzu powder (or
    cornflour)

For the dill oil
4 bunches of dill
140ml olive oil

For the poached rhubarb and gel
8 large stalks of rhubarb
600ml still mineral water
200g caster sugar
10g agar agar powder

**For the mushroom and smoked
mackerel purée**
100g button mushrooms, chilled
100g smoked mackerel fillet, skinned
    and pin-boned, then kept chilled
50ml dashi stock, chilled
½ teaspoon yuzu purée (thawed if
    frozen)
fleur de sel

To serve
4 open, brown cap mushrooms
miso purée
bronze fennel

Start with the soused mackerel. Put the fillets into a wide, shallow dish and sprinkle with rice wine vinegar. Leave for 1 minute.

Gently remove the outer membrane layer of the skin. Put the mackerel back into the dish and add more vinegar so the fish is submerged. Leave to pickle for 30 minutes.

Lift out the fish (reserve the vinegar). Remove the pin bones. Place the fillets on a tray and keep in a cool place.

Pour the reserved vinegar into a pan and bring to the boil. Mix the Japanese kuzu powder with a little water, then add to the vinegar and stir to thicken. Cool, then pour into a squeezy bottle. Reserve at room temperature.

Next make the dill oil. Pick the dill fronds from the stems. Blanch the fronds in boiling water for 30 seconds, then drain and refresh. Squeeze dry and place in a blender. With the machine running, slowly pour in the olive oil through the feed tube until all has been added. Slowly decant the oil through a sieve into a jar or bowl. Keep, covered, in the fridge.

For the poached rhubarb, peel the rhubarb (keep the peel), then cut into batons. Divide equally among four sous vide bags, but don't seal. Pour the mineral water into a saucepan, add the sugar and bring to the boil, stirring to dissolve the sugar. Stir in the rhubarb peel and infuse for 5 minutes over a low heat. Cool down rapidly by setting the pan in a bowl of iced water. Once cool, pass through a sieve, then divide the liquid evenly among the sous vide bags and seal. Place the bags in a pan of boiling water and cook briefly – no longer than 3 minutes, depending on the size of the pieces of rhubarb. Cool down rapidly, then drain, reserving the poaching liquid.

If you don't have a sous vide machine or bags, simply roast the rhubarb in the oven in the poaching liquid for 20 minutes at 180°C (conventional oven 200°C/ Gas Mark 6), before draining the juices.

Finely dice about 2 teaspoons of the rhubarb for the garnish. Keep all the rhubarb in the fridge until ready to serve.

For the rhubarb gel, pour 500ml of the rhubarb poaching liquid into a saucepan and bring to the boil. Add the agar agar powder and stir to dissolve, then boil for 10 seconds. Cool down quickly, then blitz in a blender to a smooth and silky consistency. Place in a squeezy bottle and keep at room temperature.

To make the mushroom and smoked mackerel purée, put all the chilled ingredients (including the yuzu purée) into a blender and blitz until smooth. Working quickly so the mixture does not oxidise, pass through a fine sieve, then vacuum-pack in a sous vide bag immediately.

When ready to serve, place ½ teaspoon of finely diced poached rhubarb into each brown cap mushroom. Cover with 30g of the mushroom and mackerel purée and cover this with miso purée, enough just to cover the top. Finish with 3 drops of dill oil and a sprig of bronze fennel.

Rub some rice vinegar gel into each soused mackerel fillet, evenly coating it, and finish with a sprinkling of fleur de sel. Arrange all the elements on the plates and add a design with the rhubarb and rice vinegar gels.

● ● ●

Onion and Lime Ravioli with Broad Beans and Mint

When I worked in St Tropez, one of the chefs in the restaurant made onion soup with lots of lime. I've changed the soup to ravioli but still used lime and onion. It's important to use sweet onions to help create a sweet and sour flavour. Really, the dish is a French interpretation of Asian sweet and sour food.

Serves 8

For the ravioli
1kg Grelot onions (white parts only), finely sliced
350ml fresh lime juice
16 sheets wonton pastry

For the broad bean and mint purée
400g podded, blanched and peeled broad beans
400ml still mineral water
70g mint leaves

For the lime butter emulsion
100ml fresh lime juice
100g butter, diced

For the fricassée of broad beans
40g podded, blanched and peeled broad beans
chopped mixed herbs (parsley, tarragon and chives), to garnish

To serve
tiny Moroccan mint leaves
broad bean flowers
pea shoots

Start with the ravioli. Put the onions and lime juice into a pan and slowly cook until the onions are soft, without colouring them. Pour on to a tray and leave to cool down. When cooled, drain slightly and mix well. Chill the mix in the fridge for a couple of hours.

When ready to shape the ravioli, cut the wonton sheets into 6.5cm squares. To make each raviolo, weigh out 20g of the lime/onion mix and place on a wonton piece. Fold the wonton over the filling to create a triangular shape and press to seal using a 6.5cm round cutter (you will now have a half-moon shape). Place the finished ravioli on greaseproof paper and keep in the fridge until you are ready to cook them.

For the broad bean and mint purée, quickly blanch the broad beans in the mineral water until tender. Drain, reserving the water, then tip into a blender or food processor and blitz with the mint while still warm. Pass through a fine sieve on to a tray set over ice, to cool quickly. When cool, put back in the blender, add the reserved water and blitz well. Set aside.

To make the lime butter emulsion, warm the lime juice in a small pan and whisk in the butter, a cube at a time. Pour about half of the emulsion on to a tray and reserve for the ravioli.

For the fricassée of broad beans, add the beans to the remaining lime butter emulsion in the pan, bring to the boil and cook for 1 minute. Remove from the heat and add the herbs.

When ready to serve, gently lower the ravioli into a pan of simmering water and cook for 2 minutes until the pasta is soft. Lift out with a slotted spoon on to the tray moistened with lime butter emulsion.

Put a raviolo on each plate (two ravioli if you have enough to do so) with some of the broad bean and mint purée. Garnish with a little of the fricassée of broad beans and lime butter emulsion, and finish with a salad of tiny Moroccan mint, broad bean flowers and pea shoots.

• • •

Black Treacle Tart

Treacle tart was one of the first puddings I learned to make when I came to England. I've always liked the liquorice flavour in black treacle, so I use this instead of golden treacle because it gives more depth to the tart. It's one of my wife, Lucy's, favourite desserts.

Serves 8–10

For the tart case
300g salted butter, chilled, cubed
112g caster sugar
500g plain flour
40g cornflour
1 egg plus 1 yolk
112g feuilletine flakes

For the filling
100g unsalted butter, diced
grated zest and juice of 1 lemon
85g fresh breadcrumbs
350g golden syrup
100g treacle
2 eggs plus 2 egg yolks
40ml double cream

First make the pastry. Combine the butter, sugar, flour and cornflour in the bowl of a food mixer fitted with the paddle attachment and run the machine until you have a breadcrumb consistency. Add the whole egg to bind the crumbs together. Add the feuilletine. Wrap the pastry in clingfilm and leave to rest in the fridge for at least 30 minutes.

Roll out the pastry on a lightly floured surface to 2cm thick. Use to line a 25cm fluted, loose-based tart or flan tin, then rest in the fridge again.

Preheat the oven to 170°C (conventional oven 190°C/Gas Mark 5). Line the pastry case with clingfilm and fill with baking beans, then bake blind for 20 minutes until light golden brown. Remove the baking beans and clingfilm. Brush the pastry case with the beaten egg yolk, then put back in the oven to bake for 1 or 2 more minutes (this fills in any gaps or holes in the pastry). Set the tart case aside.

Turn the oven down to 110°C (conventional oven 130°C/Gas Mark ½).

For the filling, melt the butter in a heavy-based saucepan, then gently cook, swirling the butter in the pan from time to time, until it turns a light brown and smells nutty. Remove from the heat and leave to cool slightly. Add the lemon zest and juice to the browned butter followed by the breadcrumbs and mix together. In another saucepan, gently warm the golden syrup with the treacle, just until liquified but not hot. Off the heat, beat in the eggs, yolks and cream. Fold this mix with the breadcrumb mix.

Pour into the tart case and bake for 20–30 minutes until the filling is just set. Leave to cool before slicing. Serve with ice cream or clotted cream.

• • •

Massimo
Bottura

'I think the most important ingredient to use in the kitchen is one's mind.'

Bottura

Massimo Bottura is Italy's modern magician of food. He translates the traditional flavours of his country into witty, artful, contemporary dishes – plates of food like his most famous creation, 'five textures and temperatures out of Parmigiano Reggiano'.

His passion for food was ignited as a child, watching his mother, grandmother and aunt conjuring up family meals 'under cascades of flour and Parmigiano Reggiano'. Despite this, Bottura was earmarked for a legal career; but he dropped out of law college and instead bought a trattoria on the outskirts of his hometown, Modena, in 1986.

Nine years later after training with French chefs George Coigny and Alan Ducasse, Bottura opened his world-renowned Modena restaurant, Osteria Francescana. Subsequent encouragement from the great Spanish molecular maestro Ferran Adrià set him firmly on the road to innovation – and many awards, including three-Michelin-stars and the Swedish White Guide Global Gastronomy Award in 2014. He has since opened two more restaurants – Franceschetta 58 in Modena, and Ristorante Italia di Massimo Bottura in Istanbul.

Home cooking opportunities are rare because of his work commitments, but when he cooks he reverts to traditional Italian fare – home-made egg pasta tortelloni, cotechino or veal tongue with salsa verde will often be on the table.

His home cooking environment of choice, he says, is a clean kitchen with an interesting record on the stereo (Bottura has 10,000 vinyl records); good ingredients in the pantry; friends or family around; and a good pair of sneakers (he owns hundreds of pairs) – 'You can't go wrong.'

• • •

Secret Food Haunt
Mercato Albinelli, a covered market dating from 1919, in the centre of Modena next to the main square. Stalls sell everything from dairy products with the best Italian cheeses to Italian pantry staples like olives, sardines, anchovies, baccalà, dried porcini or tomatoes, as well as fresh fruit, vegetables, meat and fish.

Riso Cacio e Pepe

A risotto with a message. This unique risotto recipe was created after the May 2012 earthquakes destroyed 350,000 wheels of Parmigiano Reggiano cheese. Vialone Nano rice is simmered in the purest Parmigiano broth infused with pepper to recreate the classic Roman cheese and pepper combination with a distinctively Emilian touch of irony and flavour.

Serves 6

500g Parmigiano Reggiano (aged 30 months)
4 litres still mineral water, at room temperature
5g white peppercorns
2.5g Sichuan peppercorns
2.5g Jamaican peppercorns (allspice berries)
2.5g black Sarawak peppercorns
2.5g wild peppercorns
500g Vialone Nano rice
1 teaspoon extra virgin olive oil

Grate the Parmigiano Reggiano and add to a pot containing the mineral water. Slowly heat until the temperature of the mixture is 80°C; do not heat to more than 90°C. When the Parmigiano becomes stringy, remove the pot from the heat. Leave the mixture to cool to room temperature, then cover and refrigerate for 24 hours.

Finely grind the peppercorns to a powder and mix them together. Put aside for finishing the plates.

The next day the Parmigiano mixture should have separated into three consistencies: creamy paste on top, milky water in the middle and solid proteins on the bottom. Separate the creamy paste (top layer) from the rest and put aside for the risotto. Filter the liquid through a sieve lined with muslin to remove the solids and make Parmigiano water; discard all the solids. Put the liquid aside for the risotto.

Toast the rice in a heavy saucepan with the olive oil. Then begin to wet the rice with the Parmigiano water, a ladleful at a time, just as you would do when making a normal risotto with stock. Let each addition of Parmigiano water be absorbed before adding the next and stir frequently. Three-quarters of the way through the cooking, begin to add the Parmigiano Reggiano cream, a tablespoon at a time. Continue stirring.

When the rice is almost done, add the rest of the Parmigiano Reggiano cream and blend gently.

Spoon a portion of the risotto on to each plate and flatten it into a disc. Add a light dusting of the pepper powder and let sit for a minute before serving.

● ● ●

Spaghetti alla Cetarese

Cetara is a fishing village on the Gulf of Naples where anchovies have been caught and cured for centuries. This unique pesto is named after it and made with the simplest ingredients found in every Italian pantry. Anchovies, parsley and pine nuts are hand chopped into a savoury sauce for spaghetti.

Serves 4

30g whole anchovies packed in salt (preferably from Cetara)

100g pine nuts

65g capers packed in salt (preferably from Pantelleria), rinsed

2.5g peeled garlic (about 1 clove)

4 teaspoons extra virgin olive oil (preferably Villa Manodori)

100g flat-leaf parsley leaves

4g fine sea salt

360g spaghetti

800ml fish stock, simmering

Remove the bone from the anchovies and quickly rinse them under cold water. Finely chop the anchovy fillets with the pine nuts and capers to make a pesto, preferably using a knife, not a blender. It is very important that the knife is sharp, to cut the ingredients finely without crushing them. Set the pesto aside, covered.

Grate the garlic and mix with 1 teaspoon of the olive oil in a large pan. Set aside.

Blanch the parsley leaves in a pan of boiling water for 20 seconds, then drain and place immediately in iced water. Drain again and pat dry with kitchen paper before blending with the remaining oil and the salt to obtain a uniform, velvety texture.

Boil the pasta in 10 litres of salted water until it is half cooked (60–70 per cent of the cooking time on the packet). Meanwhile, heat the garlic and oil mixture, then add a tablespoon of the pesto.

When the spaghetti is half cooked, drain it in a colander, then tip it into the pan containing the garlic and pesto mixture. Finish cooking over a high flame as if making a risotto, by gradually adding the simmering fish stock while stirring and adding more pesto as needed, until the pasta is perfectly cooked.

At the very end, mix well, adding the parsley oil, and then serve.

• • •

Soufflé of Panettone

Panettone is a classic Italian Christmas bread with candied fruits. Traditionally given as a housewarming present during the holidays, there is always plenty of left-over panettone from Christmas Eve that can be revived the day after into a light and fragrant soufflé.

Serves 10

600g panettone
melted butter and plain flour for the
   moulds
13 eggs, separated
150g caster sugar
200g white chocolate, broken up
95g unsalted butter

Blitz the panettone into fine crumbs in a food processor.

Preheat the oven to 180°C (conventional oven 200°C/Gas Mark 6). Brush melted butter around the inside of six small, round metal or silicone cake moulds that are 8cm across and 4cm deep. Dust the moulds lightly with flour.

Beat 12 of the egg yolks with half the sugar until pale and fluffy. (You won't need the last egg yolk).

Melt the white chocolate with the butter in a heatproof bowl set over a pan of hot water (the base of the bowl should not touch the water), or in a microwave on low to mid power (300–600W). Set aside to cool slightly.

Meanwhile, whisk the 13 egg whites with the remaining sugar until they will hold stiff peaks.

Add the melted chocolate mixture to the yolk mixture, stirring quickly to avoid the yolks getting warm. Mix in the panettone. Finally, fold in the whisked whites gently but thoroughly. Spoon into the moulds to fill by three-quarters. Bake for 10–12 minutes until risen and golden brown. Serve immediately.

• • •

Claire
Clark

'Coconut blossom sugar has great health benefits and makes wonderful cakes.'

Clark

English patissière Claire Clark is one of Britain's finest pastry chefs. The first woman to hold the highest honour of her profession in Britain, a Master of Culinary Arts, she has a career in one of the world's most iconic restaurants, California's The French Laundry, behind her and now a flourishing bespoke patisserie business, Indulge, in London. She is also the proud recipient of one of the UK's highest public honours, an MBE (Member of the British Empire).

It could all have been so different if her first job in the main kitchen of a small restaurant had been successful. 'I fainted from heat exhaustion, so decided I needed to be a pastry chef!'

Early training in the art of Swiss and German patisserie was followed by a roll call of jobs in some of London's most prestigious restaurants, including the famous Claridge's hotel. She also helped to launch the phenomenally successful grand café-restaurant, the Wolseley, before four 'inspirational' years at The French Laundry.

It was here that Clark became famous for her shortbread, given as a parting gift to diners as they left. Made with a recipe passed down from her mother, it is 'the best and simplest recipe' in her repertoire, gleaned originally in the 1960s from the back of a bag of flour.

As you'd expect with a pastry chef, her breakfast isn't always run-of-the-mill. Fruit cake, marmite and peanut butter on toast (together) or porridge in the winter set her up for a working day. 'I can't live without marmite.'

There are of course more exotic patisserie ingredients in her larder: things like coconut blossom sugar and freeze-dried fruit. When she's able to free up time to cook at home, she loves nothing better than to do a Sunday roast – and cake, naturally – for her siblings and their children: or to host dinner parties for friends.

Time off is also reserved for reading, specifically books on murder cases and forensics. 'I'm fascinated by them. I've read both volumes of the *Encyclopedia of Mass Murder* from front-to-back!' No doubt with a cup of Earl Grey tea poured out of her silver teapot at her side for reassurance.

● ● ●

Secret Food Haunt

The Cheese Cellar, a gourmet supplier in Battersea, South London that specialises in sourcing from small independent producers in the UK and Europe. In addition to cheese, other dairy produce, charcuterie and preserves are sold; as well as freeze dried-fruit from New Zealand, 'my favourite ingredient ever'.

Herrrings and Wódka

My boyfriend André, who is half Polish-half Russian, won me with this herring dish! Don't forget to serve a shot of vodka with the herrings (or to chill it and the glasses): it's a must as an accompaniment, as is toasted sour bread.

Serves 6–8

750g salted herring fillets
1 onion, finely chopped
½ eating apple, peeled and roughly chopped
1 teaspoon chopped dill, plus extra to garnish
150ml extra virgin olive oil
1 lemon, cut into 4 wedges
freshly ground black pepper

To serve
hot toasted sourdough bread
a good-quality pure rye grain Polish vodka (such as Wódka Wiborowa), well chilled in the freezer

Cut the herring fillets into small bite-sized pieces and put into a bowl. Add the chopped onion and then the apple. Mix together and season with freshly ground black pepper. Stir in the dill. Add the olive oil and stir to mix.

Put the mixture into a serving dish. Sprinkle with a little more dill and coarsely ground black pepper. Push the lemon wedges partway into the mixture. Cover and leave in a cool place such as a larder or fridge for a day or so.

Serve the herrings at room temperature with hot toasted sourdough and wash down with the cold vodka served in chilled shot glasses.

● ● ●

Koulibiac

You can prepare this classic dish the day before serving it. Just leave it in the fridge overnight and cook on the day you eat it. You can eat it cold, too. We often pack any leftovers into a hamper and head out on an impromptu picnic.

Serves 6–8

500g rough puff pastry (see below),
   or ready-made butter puff pastry,
   thawed if frozen
1 egg, beaten

For the filling
15g dried porcini mushrooms
60g basmati rice
¼ teaspoon ground turmeric
1 onion, diced
60g butter
175g shiitake or button mushrooms,
   chopped
700g skinless cooked salmon, flaked
   (smoked haddock can be used
   as an alternative)
2 tablespoons chopped dill
2 tablespoons chopped parsley
2 hard-boiled eggs, shelled and
   chopped
salt and freshly ground black pepper

For the rough puff pastry
500g strong white flour
10g salt
500g unsalted butter, cut into cubes

Begin by making the pastry. Sift the flour and salt on to a cool work surface (preferably a marble slab) and make a large well in the centre (the well should be wide and shallow rather than deep). Place the cubes of butter in the well and, using your fingertips, lightly work the ingredients together, gradually drawing in the flour. When the cubes of butter have broken up and become slightly flattened, add 250ml cold water to the well and gradually mix all the ingredients together. Do not knead the dough, and stop working it as soon as it becomes homogeneous. It should still contain visible flakes of butter.

Clean the marble slab and flour it lightly. Roll out the dough away from you to a rectangle three times as long as it is wide. Fold up one third of the dough, then fold down the remaining third on top to make three layers. Make sure the block is neat and precise with square edges. Give it a quarter turn so the folded edges are to your right and left. This is your first 'turn'.

Now roll out the pastry away from you again into a rectangle three times as long as it is wide and about 1cm thick (as you are rolling, dust the work surface regularly with flour and pick up the pastry to make sure it is not sticking). Fold it into three as before. Wrap in clingfilm and rest in the fridge for 20 minutes.

Repeat the rolling and folding process twice more, to make four 'turns' in total. Wrap the pastry well in clingfilm and chill for 1 hour before using. (This makes 1.25kg pastry, more than you need for the Koulibiac; you can store the unused pastry in the fridge for a couple of days or in the freezer for up to 3 months).

To make the filling, soak the dried porcini in hot water for 30 minutes. Pick out the mushroom pieces and chop fairly finely. (Keep the soaking liquid to add to a soup or stock).

Cook the rice with the turmeric in a pan of lightly salted boiling water until just al dente. Drain thoroughly and set aside. Sweat the onion in the butter until tender. Add the fresh mushrooms and the soaked porcini and cook until all the liquid from the fresh mushrooms has evaporated, leaving a moist mush in the pan. Tip this into a bowl and add the rice, salmon, herbs and hard-boiled eggs. Season generously with salt and pepper.

Roll out the 500g pastry on a lightly floured board to form a rectangle about 35 x 45cm. Transfer to a lightly greased baking sheet. Mound the filling down the centre of the pastry, patting it to form an even, fat sausage shape.

Brush the edges of the long sides of the pastry with beaten egg, then lift them up and over the filling, pressing together to seal. Seal the ends with beaten egg, folding the joins towards the long central seam. Gently roll the koulibiac over on the baking sheet so the seam is underneath. Brush the koulibiac all over with the remainder of the beaten egg. If you wish, you can decorate with pretty pastry shapes. Leave to rest for 30 minutes before baking.

Preheat the oven to 200°C (conventional oven 220°C/Gas Mark 7). Bake the koulibiac for 40–45 minutes until golden brown and flaky. Serve either hot or cold.

● ● ●

Lemon and Thyme Trifle

Herbs are great additions to salads and savoury dishes, but I like to use them in desserts and pâtisserie too as their fragrance enhances fruity flavours. Lemon and thyme work particularly well together. There are quite a few components to this dramatic and delicate dessert, but everything comes together so beautifully and it is worth the extra effort. You will need tube-shaped moulds: I use cannoli moulds lined with acetate.

Serves 6

For the lemon and thyme custard
2 gelatine leaves
250ml milk
2 large sprigs of thyme
grated zest of 1 lemon
2 egg yolks
90g caster sugar
240ml double cream

For the almond sponge
160g unsalted butter, at room
    temperature
150g caster sugar
4 small eggs
20g plain flour
160g ground almonds
20g cornflour
grated zest of 1 lemon

For the simple syrup
50g caster sugar

For the lemon curd
2 eggs
80g caster sugar
55ml lemon juice
100g unsalted butter

For the lemon curd jelly
2.5g agar agar powder

For the crème chantilly
½ vanilla pod
100ml double cream
10g icing sugar

For the lemon syrup
100g caster sugar
juice of 2 lemons

For the decoration
sprigs of thyme
small edible flowers

Start with the custard. Prepare three cannoli or other tube-shaped moulds, each about 14cm long and 2cm in diameter, by lining the inside of each with a piece of acetate, to cover. The acetate ensures easy removal of the custard. (If you don't have acetate, lightly oil the cannoli moulds with flavourless groundnut oil).

Soak the gelatine leaves in cold water for 10 minutes to soften, then remove from the water and squeeze dry. Leave on one side.

Bring the milk to the boil with the thyme and lemon zest. Meanwhile, mix together the egg yolks and sugar in a bowl. Pour the hot milk on to the egg mixture, whisking to combine. Pour back into the pan and cook on a low heat, stirring continuously, until the custard coats the back of the spoon. Take care not to let the custard boil or it will curdle.

Remove from the heat, add the soaked gelatine leaves and stir until they have melted. Pass the custard through a sieve into a clean bowl. Leave on one side to cool until the custard starts to thicken. Whip the cream to soft peaks, then fold into the setting custard. Chill the custard in the fridge for at least an hour.

Spoon into a piping bag and pipe into the prepared moulds. Chill until fully set, then transfer the moulds to the freezer so that the custards become very firm. Once frozen, remove the custard tubes from their acetate-lined moulds and lay them on a tray lined with baking parchment. Keep in the freezer until ready to serve.

For the almond sponge, preheat the oven to 160°C (conventional oven 180°C/ Gas Mark 4). Use baking parchment to line a 15 x 10cm rectangular tin that is 2.5cm deep.

Cream the butter with the sugar until pale and fluffy. Gradually beat in one of the eggs. Sift the flour, ground almonds and cornflour together, then fold into the cake mixture. Beat the remaining eggs together to mix, then add to the cake mixture. Mix well, then fold in the grated lemon zest.

Transfer the cake mixture to the prepared tin and level the surface. Bake for 18–20 minutes until the sponge is well risen and golden, and will spring back when lightly pressed. Cool in the tin. When cold, place in the freezer to chill and firm up.

To make the simple syrup, dissolve the sugar in 50ml water and bring to the boil, then remove from the heat and leave to cool.

For the lemon curd, put all the ingredients in a heatproof bowl set over a pan of gently simmering water (the base of the bowl should not touch the water). Whisk until the curd thickens and will leave a trail on its surface when the whisk is lifted. Pass the curd through a fine sieve into a clean bowl and leave to cool.

When the simple syrup and lemon curd are cool, make the lemon curd jelly. Put the curd and syrup in a pan and bring to the boil. Scatter in the agar agar while

whisking. Bring back to a simmer and cook for 3 minutes, whisking all the time. Pass through a chinois (fine sieve) on to a flat tray to make a thin 2mm layer. Leave the jelly to set before moving the tray. Chill in the fridge to firm up.

Now make the crème chantilly. Slit the vanilla pod in half along its length and remove the seeds with the point of a knife. Add to the cream with the sifted icing sugar and whip until it will hold soft peaks. Keep in the fridge until needed.

For the lemon syrup, dissolve the sugar in the lemon juice and bring to the boil, then remove from the heat. Leave to cool in the pan.

When you are ready to start assembling the dessert, remove the custard tubes from the freezer and the jelly from the fridge. Cut each tube across in half. Cut the jelly into rectangles, each just the right size to wrap completely around a custard log. The jelly should be an exact fit so it's best to use a ruler to measure. Transfer the jelly-wrapped custard logs to a small tray and keep in the fridge.

Next, cut six rectangles, each 7.5 x 2.5cm, from the cooled almond sponge. Every rectangle should be even and level, so use a knife to shave off some of the centre part if necessary.

Reheat the lemon syrup until warm. Carefully dunk each sponge rectangle in the syrup so it absorbs as much as possible without falling apart. Set the sponges on a small tray lined with baking parchment and chill to firm up a bit.

To serve, set each syrup-soaked sponge on a plate and place a jelly-wrapped custard log on top at an angle. Check the consistency of the crème chantilly and whip briefly if necessary before piping five neat blobs on to each plate. Decorate the plate with thyme and flowers.

• • •

Wylie
Dufresne

'Keep it simple, always.'

Dufresne

Wylie Dufresne has been cooking experimental and thought-provoking food in New York City for more than a decade, constantly challenging dining preconceptions and earning himself the tag of being America's leading proponent of molecular gastronomy in the process.

Always the kid who 'asked the extra question' at school, it's no surprise that his enquiring mind led him to explore and experiment with the scientific processes behind cooking at his much-lauded restaurant WD-50, on New York's Lower East Side (which sadly closed at the end of 2014 due to its site being redeveloped).

But his earliest brush with the culinary world came through his father, Dewey, who owned sandwich shops in Rhode Island, later becoming the inspiration behind the WD-50 signature dish of deconstructed tongue sandwich, with fried mayonnaise (bound with hydrocolloids) and sweet tomato molasses.

Before he carved his own singular culinary path, though, Dufresne attended New York's French Culinary Institute and extended his culinary education by working for five years in the kitchens of the great Jean-Georges Vongerichten ('still an inspiration after 20 years!').

WD-50 opened in 2003, immediately causing a stir with its adventurous cooking. It wasn't long before witty dishes like amaro duck yolk (cured for six hours) with chicken confit won fame beyond the restaurant's doors, even beyond the USA. When Michelin launched its inaugural New York guide in 2006, WD-50 bagged a star. In addition, Dufresne is a winner of one of the USA's most prestigious hospitality accolades, a James Beard award (2013 Best New York City Chef).

Secret Food Haunt
Joe Coffee in Union Square, New York City. Not food, but 'the best coffee in NYC' is served here. It's one of a chain of 10 Joe Coffee outlets in New York City and Philadelphia. Founded in 2003, the company roasts its own beans – both single-origin estate and blended beans – and is committed to Fair Trade and produce traceability.

WD-50's success meant Dufresne was able to launch a sister New York restaurant, Alder, in 2013, which kept him busy after the former closed. But when work allows, he checks out new hotspots in New York or old haunts such as PDT (Please Don't Tell) cocktail bar.

At home, on the whole, he takes a break from cooking: scrambled eggs, cereal with very cold milk, or manning the grill if there's grilling to be done is about his limit ('my wife is a really good cook'). That said, he's not averse to raiding the larder for a packet of that most traditional of American cookies, Graham crackers: 'We're never without them – the kids love them!'

• • •

Egg Sandwich, Buffet Done Right

I don't do a lot of cooking at home. But I do enjoy cooking for my family and when at home I tend to keep things pretty simple. When cooking at home it is usually for small numbers – often times just my wife and me. One of my go-to favourites is breakfast! I have had a certain degree of success among family and friends when it comes to my breakfast. And I love eggs, of course. So certainly one dish I'm known for is eggs benedict. I make that every New Year's Eve morning for my staff at the restaurant, and it is a big hit.

But really, one of my best 'standards' in the breakfast arena – the one I often go to – is the breakfast sandwich, which is simply scrambled eggs on an English muffin, with cheese (usually American) and bacon. I will also, in the style of a proper buffet, put fruit out – sliced fruit, melon, berries, yoghurt. Beverages are also key, so we'll have juice, sparkling water that we make in-house and iced coffee. I'm a big fan of iced coffee.

I learned how to scramble eggs from the French. And that historically meant loosely scrambled eggs. Or what we would call a soft scramble. And for many years I followed that same routine, which meant putting some butter in a pan, beating the eggs and seasoning with salt and cayenne (I always put a pinch of cayenne in my eggs, even though I don't like spicy food; it is something I learned early on and it has stuck with me), and then scrambling the eggs. And you wouldn't want a really hot pan when you first start. You would start out more slowly on a medium heat, and let the butter get foamy. Then you add your eggs and stir with a long, narrow sauce whisk. And just work slowly. It is a long process, the French way. And what happens is you begin to cook the eggs so slowly that you get very small curds in a kind of sea of cooked egg.

However, I've changed the way I cook the eggs. I realised it is better for sandwiches – and ultimately gives you a little more leeway – to cook the egg a little harder. But remember, you still have to keep whisking! A lot! Just turn the heat up a little higher and move the pan on and off the heat. You will still want to aim for those tiny curds. It should begin to resemble cottage cheese in texture.

Eventually you can whisk in cheese – goat's cheese, brie, jack, etc. But again, for me, it is American cheese. It is a perfect melt, after all.

Many years ago I came across the trick of using cream cheese, which of course melts magically. So I have now taken to adding a little bit of cream cheese at the very end. You don't need a lot. Add the cheese – cream and American or otherwise – at the end once you've taken the pan off the heat. The heat of the eggs will melt the cheese, and the cheese will keep the egg from cooking any further. And when you are done, you have eggs that are much better suited for a sandwich.

I will usually put these scrambled eggs on a toasted English muffin, and perhaps add some bacon. (I am a fan of the bacon press. Everyone has a different take on their bacon preferences, but I like to use the press. I like my bacon flat). You can also gild the lily and add another piece of cheese (American) on top and give it a quick flash in the oven. Definitely make more than one per person.

Alternatively, serve up the scrambled eggs in a big bowl with a stack of toast. My mother-in-law makes a delicious cinnamon-raisin toast, which we have on the menu at Alder under the name 'Grandma Toast'. I myself am also a fan of rye toast. But of course the English muffin is classic.

However you arrange all the elements, everyone can agree on these as the staples of breakfast!

• • •

Frozen Pea Purée and Rabbit Pasta

Pastas are good family-style dishes.

The funny thing is that, for me, even when I am at home I will 'plate' all the dishes. It is just a habit. There was one particularly amusing moment when, on Christmas day at my in-laws' house, there was not enough counter space to set out plates for all 12 people. I was making eggs benedict. So I put a dozen plates on their floor, and the family watched me as I crouched to plate everything on the kitchen tile floor.

Pasta, though, is great for avoiding the plating conundrums like that and embracing the family-style service.

There is one pasta that I have been making for many years. It starts with a pea purée. Using frozen peas (because those are the best for puréeing), put most of the peas in a blender, reserving a cup or two for later. The quality of the blending will affect the outcome of the product. So the first thing I might do is put the peas in a colander and run some water over them, just to soften them a bit.

Add a little water to the peas, and really purée them. I like a very smooth pea purée. And you want it fairly loose, in my opinion. Everyone has a different preference, but just keep in mind that this is going to be the sauce for your pasta. So you probably want it thinner than you think. And season to taste. You can add a little salt, a little pepper, a little olive oil. I tend to keep it fairly clean. But once blended and seasoned, reserve the sauce until needed.

I like to make this dish with rabbit legs, which you will need to confit. So take the meat and set it in some sort of container to cook it – perhaps a casserole dish. Season with salt and pepper, cover it with a little oil or some clarified butter, and throw some spices like thyme, garlic and bay leaf in there with it. You want the oil and/or butter to cover the rabbit. This can be a lot, depending on how many legs you might be making. But keep in mind that this fat can be used for other things – sautéing potatoes, cooking with, in vinaigrettes. That oil will become very flavourful.

It will take 2–3 hours at a very low heat to confit. You do not want the oil to bubble, because that means you are actually pulling the water out of the rabbit. Oil has no water in it, obviously, so if you see that consistent bubbling, that is the water trying to escape. All you want to see is the occasional break in the oil.

At the end of this process, the goal is to be able to grab the leg bone and pretty easily pull it right out. I do think it is a fine line between cooked and overcooked – and perhaps better to err on the side of caution and cook more than less – but overcooked rabbit is like cat food. So you want the rabbit to be very much like a well-cooked chicken where the meat tears off easily in big pieces. If you grab the bone and it comes flying out, start over. Or make rabbit roux.

Let the meat cool until you can handle it and then gently pick the meat off the bone. Discard the bone.

Put a pot of water on the stove in preparation to cook the pasta.

In the meantime you want to think about the other element for the pasta. What I like in this case are mushrooms. And the mushrooms can really be of your choosing – whether you want to get some nice chanterelles and splurge, or if you just want to use shiitakes and white buttons. I don't like portabello mushrooms, but if you do, go for it!

Any time you cook a vegetable, you want to make sure all of them are more or less the same size. So if you are getting different kinds, break them down until the sizes are consistent. And I will generally use a large sauté pan, or something

of that sort. If you have a lid, that is great. You'll just want to put a little butter in the pan, and then add all of the mushrooms. I like to take a finely sliced shallot (maybe 1–2, depending on your taste) and throw it in with the mushrooms, along with some salt and white pepper. And I would also put a little water in there. I know people will think mushrooms should be letting go of their water when they are cooked. But a little water in the pan with the lid on, over the heat, will turn to steam and it will cook the mushrooms faster. It will look soupy, but that is ok. And once it has that soupy consistency, you'll want to take the lid off and cook the mushrooms down. When I do it, I like to take the mushrooms down until they are dry and you see some brown on the bottom of the pan. Then I'll add a splash more water and using a spatula I will scrape those bits from the bottom of the pan and get that incorporated back into the mushrooms. I'll bring it down and let it caramelise again, then will again deglaze with a splash of water. Do this three or four times, and you will get a much deeper mushroom flavour.

At this point, you will want to fire your pasta. In this case, I like cavatelli which is the long and narrow pasta that looks kind of like a canoe. Orzo is also really nice if you'd like. Anything that will grab the sauce well. For this dish you probably do not want a long noodle like spaghetti. Whatever you choose, cook the pasta as you normally would and drain (saving a little of the pasta water).

Now the biggest pot you probably have at your disposal – and what is now hot from the stove – is the pasta pot. So I would throw the mushrooms into that pot, followed by half the pasta. Start adding the pea purée, stirring it as you go, then add the rest of the pasta. Again, you may find that you need to add some water (use the pasta water) to give a nice consistency to the sauce. You are trying to create something like a tomato sauce, but in this case it is bright green.

Then add the peas that you set aside and a knob of butter or a bit of olive oil. Mix that all in. Once everything is mixed to your liking, season with salt and freshly ground pepper. Add the rabbit last. Wait until the end to add the rabbit because you will want the meat to stay in nice, large chunks.

To finish, I will usually put everything into a big serving dish with toasted breadcrumbs, fresh mint and fresh basil on top. Serve and enjoy!

. . .

Wylie's Roast Chicken

At home, I find that I'm often making chicken. Just classic, roasted chicken. And I love roasting whole chickens, but the way I have come to favour cooking chicken at home is to just do the thighs. Boneless, skin-on chicken thighs. Not the drum, just the thigh. Roasting a whole chicken takes a while and it is great because there are always leftovers. But if I'm cooking for my wife, I'll just do the thighs.

The thigh is the best part of the chicken. It has the most flavour. Chicken breasts, I feel bad for. Even if it's done right, and super juicy with crispy skin, the breast is never more than adequate. But a proper chicken thigh is delicious. THAT is ethereal to me!

For me it is simple – cast-iron pan on the stove, over a high heat, a little bit of clarified butter. Well, I should mention that when I'm cooking at home, I'm often doing my 'shopping' at my restaurant. So I can bring home clarified butter without any problem. But I digress…

Season the thighs with salt and white pepper. Then remove the pan from the flame and, away from the heat, just lay the thighs in the pan. But make sure to lay them down in a motion going away from yourself. Many people make the mistake of laying things in a hot pan of butter or oil coming towards their body. That is bad. The oil or butter can splash up and burn your arm. But now you've been warned.

Four thighs will feed two people and will all fit in a cast-iron pan.

At that point, you'll want to turn down the heat immediately to just south of medium. And you want the cooking to take a little while because you want that skin to get a little crispy. Then you'll want to add a little bit of garlic (1 or 2 cloves, unpeeled and smashed) and a handful of thyme.

You will know when the thighs are about 80–85 per cent done, as the skin is nice and golden brown and the colouring is starting to come up from the bottom around the edges, working its way to the top. At that point, you still don't want to flip the thighs over. People often do that, but I think it dries the meat out. You just want to add a nice knob of butter to the pan with the aromatics. It will start to sizzle and pop. Then take the pan off the heat, tilt the pan ever so slightly and begin to baste the top of the thighs. Just pour that hot, flavoured butter over the chicken for a minute or two. It will begin to cook from the top.

THEN, turn all the thighs over, shut the heat off and count to ten. Immediately take them out and put on a plate to rest for 10 minutes, before checking they are cooked through.

Now it is time to talk about the garnish. There are a lot of different ways to go, but I love mashed potatoes with roast chicken. There's nothing terribly fancy about it. I personally like a blend of starchy and waxy potatoes. So maybe 60 per cent Idaho and 40 per cent Yukon. But that's pretty picky!

Peel your potatoes and get them more or less the same size. Put them in a pot of water and bring up the heat until the water starts to boil. Then right away bring the water down to a simmer. You don't need to have the water at a full boil. If it boils, the potatoes will begin to swell and take on water. You want them to cook gently. You aren't helping the process by cooking them at a higher temperature.

Once the potatoes are done (check with a fork! There's no secret here!), drain them. After draining the potatoes, you are left with the big hot pot that they were just cooked in. So add a little butter and a little light cream into that pot. The heat of it will begin to melt the butter and warm the cream. Then I like to use a food mill or ricer over that pot to grate/mash the potatoes. Of course, you can

also mash them the old-fashioned way. But again, be careful of the hot butter splashing up at you. It is a lesson you don't need to learn the hard way.

Turn the heat on very low and at that point add some salt, and perhaps some additional butter or cream. You should really do it to your taste. Some people like their potatoes stiffer, others like them looser. But it is worth noting that, either way, potatoes always require more seasoning than you think they will. So keep checking and adding salt to taste. I like to add white pepper, just in small quantities.

I think it is nice to use simple greens to finish off the dish. Something like romaine hearts or endive (chicory), that are lightly dressed in a simple vinaigrette (a little mustard, red wine vinegar, olive oil). I like the endive because it is bitter and I like the romaine because of its nice watery crunch. Both have a lot of texture, and even when I'm cooking at home I like to play with texture. The other great thing about using these kinds of leafy vegetables is that they are sturdy and hearty. And they complete the picture of the entire meal on a single plate. I personally prefer to have my salad on the same plate, rather than on a separate dish, so that all of the elements can talk to each other.

Stack the chicken up against the mound of potatoes, and then stick some of those greens in there to make the family picture just right.

Again, I do steal from my own restaurant. So as the last accent I will usually bring home some chicken jus. Certainly this is harder for most people cooking at home. But I will take a little of that jus, put it in a small pot and then add the juices that came off from cooking the chicken and heat the whole thing up to make a very flavourful addition. It won't be that very clean jus that you look for in a restaurant. It has more of that rustic vibe.

And like a little kid, I like to make a volcano out of my potatoes and put some sauce in there.

For dessert, my wife makes home-made ice cream sandwiches. She uses store-bought chocolate wafers and a variety of ice creams. It's delicious!

• • •

E

Graham
Elliot

'I always say, cooking isn't what I do, it's what I am.'

Elliot

A self-styled 'army brat' who experienced a nomadic childhood, Seattle-born chef and restaurateur Graham Elliot decided early on that academia was not for him: and like many a chef before him, he started his life in hospitality almost by default, at the bottom of the culinary ladder, aged 17, as a dishwasher and table clearer.

Having discovered a fascination with the restaurant life and food, he went on to train at culinary school and eventually found his way to Chicago, where he fine-tuned his skills working for the late, great Charlie Trotter, among others. However, even before this, he had already announced his arrival on the USA's culinary scene after being named as one of the 10 New Chefs of 2004 by America's *Food and Wine* magazine while working in Vermont.

An ebullient personality in trademark white glasses, it was inevitable that Elliot would find a larger audience on the small screen. He did so in 2007 when he was narrowly beaten by the flamboyant resident 'Iron Chef' Bobby Flay in a culinary showdown on the American version of the cult television show. He went on to appear in other cookery shows, most notably as a regular judge on the American version of *MasterChef Junior* and *MasterChef*.

As a restaurateur and chef, he's always striven for a perfect marriage of gastronomy and bistro, no more so than at his first eponymous restaurant, which he opened in Chicago in 2008; within a year of its opening it had received two stars from Michelin and three from the *Chicago Tribune*.

Unsurprisingly, Elliot looks for the same enjoyment and laid-back atmosphere when he spends time eating with family and friends. He cooks 'eggies – every morning' for his three sons and reserves Sundays for the boys and wife, Allie.

Inspiringly, after losing 68kg in weight in 2013, he – together with Allie – went on to run the Chicago marathon.

In the kitchen, he's never without an offset spatula or granola in the store cupboard. And he also likes to remind everyone of undervalued ingredients, bananas for example: 'people forget how amazing their history is and how important they are to cultures around the world. I like them in both sweet and savoury preparations.'

• • •

Secret Food Haunt
West Loop Salumi, a charcuterie specialist located in the Near West Side district of Chicago is a salami lover's paradise. Its air-dried artisan charcuterie is made on site and includes bresaola, coppa, guanciale, culattello and Iberico lardo: all made from impeccably sourced, often rare-breed, meat.

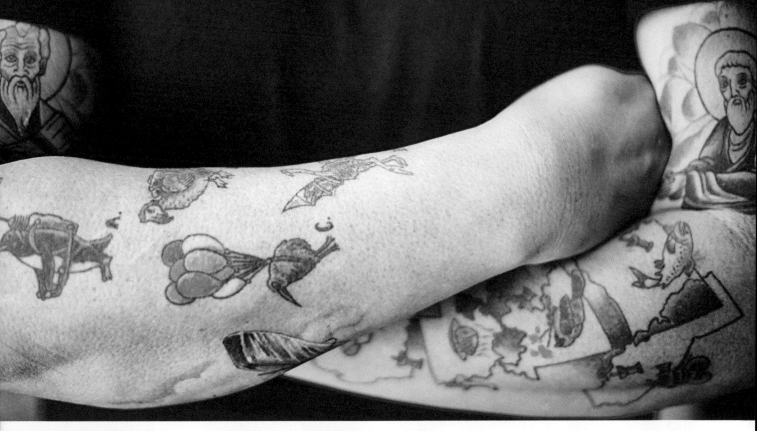

Pea Bisque with Lavender Crème Fraîche and a Pea Tendril Salad

This bisque is a beautiful way to showcase the simple essence of peas.
It makes for a wonderful spring dish to celebrate the thaw of winter.

Serves 6

For the pea bisque
500g frozen peas
200g chopped onions
20g chopped shallots
1–3 green/wet garlic cloves, chopped
olive oil
450ml full-fat milk
150ml whipping cream
225g fresh spinach leaves

For the lavender crème fraîche
250ml whipping cream
2 sprigs of lavender
200ml crème fraîche

For the dressing
¾ teaspoon pink peppercorns
1/3 teaspoon Dijon mustard
juice of 2 lemons
100ml extra virgin olive oil

For the salad
pea tendrils
pea shoots
edible flowers
chive blossoms, optional
freeze-dried peas
crushed pink peppercorns
salt and freshly ground black pepper

First make the bisque. Blanch the peas in boiling water for 3–5 minutes. Drain and refresh in cold water; set aside. Sweat the onions, shallots and green garlic in a splash of olive oil in a large saucepan until translucent, stirring occasionally.

Pour the milk and cream into the pan, stir and bring to a simmer. Reduce by half. Remove from the heat. Add half of the peas to the soup base, then blend with a hand blender (or in batches in a blender). For a very smooth bisque, pass it through a sieve. Transfer the soup to a metal container and set in an ice bath to chill quickly.

Meanwhile, blanch the spinach in boiling water for 30 seconds until soft, then drain and shock in iced water to keep the bright green colour. Drain well. Blend with the remaining peas to make a smooth purée, then add to the cold soup and stir to amalgamate. Season to taste with salt and pepper. (The bisque can be kept in the fridge for up to 2 days).

To make the lavender crème fraîche, heat the whipping cream with the lavender in a saucepan, then simmer on a very low heat until reduced to about a quarter of the original quantity. Leave to cool completely. Whip the crème fraîche with an electric mixer until very thick. Add the lavender cream with salt and pepper to taste and mix well. Keep in a cool place.

For the dressing, blend the pink peppercorns, Dijon mustard and lemon juice together in a blender or food processor. Slowly add the olive oil through the feed tube. Season to taste.

Drizzle the dressing over the salad ingredients and season with salt, then toss to mix. Serve the salad and lavender crème fraîche with the soup, or pile the salad in the centre of each bowl, place dollops of lavender crème fraîche around the salad and ladle the bisque into the bowls.

• • •

Berkshire Pork Chop with Sweet Potato Latkes and Cinnamon-spiced Apple

Sometimes, regardless of how juicy your pork is, it needs help, which apples are always happy to provide. A little spice lends some much-needed background flavour; the latkes tie the dish together and, along with autumnal sweet potatoes, provide the perfect balance of sweet and savoury.

Serves 4

4 pork chops, 280–340g each
sea salt and freshly cracked black
    pepper

For the brine
290g kosher or sea salt
100g sugar
1 tea bag
3 cardamom pods
6 black peppercorns
6 coriander seeds
2 bay leaves

For the sweet potato latkes
900g peeled sweet potatoes
1 small onion, peeled
2 teaspoons fine sea salt
3 eggs, beaten
25g sliced spring onions
3 tablespoons plain flour
vegetable oil for frying

For the cinnamon-spiced apples
2 eating apples, preferably Jonagold or
    Honeycrisp
30g unsalted butter
1 Ceylon cinnamon stick
120ml cider
120ml lager, preferably German
fine sea salt

First make the brine. Combine all the ingredients in a pot, add 2 litres water and bring to a simmer. Strain into a large shallow dish and leave to cool. Place the pork chops in the brine, side by side, and refrigerate overnight.

The next day, prepare the barbecue. While it is heating up, make the latkes and spiced apples. To make the latkes, use a box grater to grate the sweet potatoes and onion into a large mixing bowl. Season with the salt. Fold in the eggs and spring onions. Sprinkle the flour over the potato mixture and fold in with your hands.

Heat a 1cm layer of oil in a frying pan until it is hot. Fry the latkes in batches – you should be able to fit about five in the pan, depending on its size. Using your hands, scoop up a spoonful of the potato mixture and squeeze out the excess liquid, then place carefully in the hot oil. Fry for 2–3 minutes on each side until golden brown. Remove the latkes with a slotted spoon and drain on a tray lined with kitchen paper. Keep hot in a warm oven.

For the cinnamon-spiced apples, peel the apples, cut into wedges and remove the cores. Melt the butter with the cinnamon stick in a frying pan. Add the apples and gently brown in the warm butter. Pour in the cider and beer and bring to the boil. Simmer until the liquid has evaporated and the apples are glazed. Remove from the heat and season the apples with salt. Keep warm.

Remove the chops from the brine and rinse them, then pat dry with kitchen paper. Barbecue over a medium–high flame for about 6 minutes on each side or until cooked to your taste. Alternatively you can cook them in a ridged cast-iron grill pan. Season with salt and pepper.

Serve the chops with the latkes and spiced apples.

• • •

Sweet Potato with Maple Syrup and Toasted Pecans

This is a dish I've had on the menu for a while now. It screams autumn/fall with its use of maple syrup and sweet potatoes. If it's extra cold outside I might make it a little chunkier so that it's more hearty. If you prefer you can substitute either pumpkin or butternut squash for the sweet potato.

Serves 4–6

4 tablespoons orange juice
1 star anise
1 cinnamon stick
120ml pure maple syrup
5 medium-sized sweet potatoes
1 tablespoon salt
115g pecan nuts, toasted and chopped

Combine the orange juice, star anise, cinnamon and maple syrup in a bowl.

Peel the sweet potatoes and cut into 2.5cm-thick rounds. Put the sweet potatoes in a slow cooker, sprinkle with the salt and cover with the maple syrup mixture. Set the cooker to low and cook for about 6 hours until the sweet potatoes are fork tender.

Remove the cinnamon and star anise, and garnish the potatoes with the toasted pecans.

• • •

Andrew
Fairlie

'I always listen to music when I cook at home.'

Fairlie

I t's not every chef who can claim to be a judo expert. But Scotland's most famous culinary son, Andrew Fairlie, can – he even represented Scotland as a junior. From the age of nine until he began his culinary training it was a big part of his life, but then his career took over and he had to give the martial arts up.

Today, his life revolves around his eponymous restaurant at Scotland's famous Gleneagles hotel in Perthshire, which he opened to great acclaim in 2001. Over the years, his cooking – an elegant, modern interpretation of French cuisine with contemporary flavour nuances (seawood is a particular, recent, 'revelation') – has won awards galore, including two-Michelin-stars, and, from the internationally recognised Relais & Chateâux organisation, the title of Grande Chef du Monde.

It's fitting that Fairlie's restaurant is in Perthshire, his home county, as it was here he first became fascinated by the restaurant business after landing a part-time job, aged 15, as a washer-upper-come-waiter. Seduced by the excitement of the kitchen and a growing obsession with food, as soon as school exams were done he got himself into a local catering college, finished his training in London, then entered and won a competition that changed his life: the UK's famous Roux Scholarship.

Part of the prize was to spend time working with one of France's great chefs, Michel Guérard, in the south of France. It cemented Fairlie's future as a fine-dining chef and one of his most treasured possessions is a book Guérard gave to him, which bears an inscription to his protégé: 'simple food, brilliantly done'.

Fairlie follows that advice in his restaurant and at home. He always has Sundays off (having promised himself this perk once he established his own restaurant) and often cooks for his partner and daughters. Risotto is a firm family favourite: especially one made from mushrooms picked in the woods nearby. And, as with many UK chefs, Israeli chef Yotam Ottolenghi's books are a kitchen fixture.

If he were to ever open a second restaurant, don't bet against it being in Glencoe on Scotland's west coast. 'Everything I love to cook with is right there literally on my doorstep. It is spectacularly beautiful – it feels very spiritual to me.'

• • •

Secret Food Haunt

Ondine, a seafood restaurant in Edinburgh situated just off the city's famous Royal Mile. Fish and seafood is sourced from Scotland and the rest of the British Isles and the cooking is famous for being simple but elegant. 'Our favourite place for Sunday lunch.'

Rooster Potato, Smoked Pancetta and Gruyère Cake

For me, this is almost a meal on its own – served with a mixed salad, it's a perfect winter supper dish. The Red Rooster is a potato that reminds me of the potatoes I ate as a child. It's great for all sorts of things – baking, mashing, roasting and, my staff's favourite, chips.

Serves 6

1kg peeled Rooster potatoes
50g clarified unsalted butter, melted
300g smoked pancetta, very thinly sliced
350g mature Gruyère cheese
salt and freshly ground black pepper

Preheat the oven to 180°C (conventional oven 200°C/Gas Mark 6).

Evenly slice the potatoes about 3mm thick, then rinse them and dry on a clean cloth. Brush the inside of an ovenproof frying pan, about 22.5cm diameter, with a little of the melted clarified butter. Line the pan with pancetta slices, arranging them so they are slightly overlapping in a spiral pattern and leaving at least a 2cm overhang. (You should have some pancetta left over for the top).

Layer potatoes in the pan until it is a third full, then sprinkle with a layer of grated Gruyère cheese and season lightly. Repeat the layers until the pan is full, finishing with a final layer of potatoes.

Sprinkle the rest of the melted clarified butter over the potatoes. Fold the pancetta overhang on to the potatoes and use the remaining pancetta to completely cover the top.

Set the pan on the hob on a high heat to start the cooking process. When you see the pancetta start to sizzle around the edge, transfer the pan to the oven. Cook for 30 minutes. Reduce the temperature to 160°C (conventional oven 180°C/Gas Mark 4) and continue to cook for 30–40 minutes until the potatoes are tender.

Leave the potato cake to rest in the pan for 15 minutes before carefully turning out on to a plate. Cut into wedges to serve.

● ● ●

Roast Duck with Honey and Spices

This dish tastes and smells of winter and Christmas. I love the aroma of the honey and spices on a cold Sunday afternoon. Served with roasted potatoes cooked in duck fat alongside a vinegary tossed salad, it adds up to my idea of a perfect Sunday roast.

Serves 4

1 x 1.8kg duck
2 tablespoons vegetable oil
4 carrots, cut in half
2 onions, quartered
150g acacia honey
1 star anise
1 cinnamon stick, crushed into small
   pieces
½ tablespoon juniper berries
½ tablespoon black peppercorns
½ tablespoon coriander seeds
seeds from ½ tablespoon green
   cardamom pods, crushed
½ teaspoon coffee beans
2 tablespoons cider vinegar
sea salt and freshly ground
   black pepper

Preheat the oven to 220°C (conventional oven 240°C/Gas Mark 9).

Season the duck generously inside and out with salt and pepper. Lightly oil a roasting tray large enough to take the duck comfortably and place the duck in the tray on its side so it's resting on one leg. Scatter the carrots and onions around the duck, using these to prop up the duck if necessary. Roast for 30 minutes.

Meanwhile, heat the honey in a saucepan and, as it begins to boil, add the star anise, cinnamon, juniper, peppercorns, coriander, cardamom seeds and coffee beans. Mix well together. Remove from the heat, cover and set aside.

Remove the tray from the oven. Turn the duck on to its other side and, with a spoon, remove as much fat from the roasting tray as possible, leaving any juices in the tray. Return to the oven to roast for a further 20 minutes.

Remove from the oven again. Lift the duck on to a plate and cut off the legs. Tip the vegetables and cooking juices into a sieve set over a jug or bowl and strain the juices (discard the vegetables). Skim off as much fat as you can from the juices, then set aside.

Return the duck, breast side up, to the tray together with the legs. Coat the breasts with the honey mixture. Return to the oven to roast for 10 minutes, basting with the honey mixture every few minutes.

Remove the duck breast from the oven and place upside down on a plate. Cover loosely with foil and leave to rest while you continue to roast the legs for a further 10–15 minutes. After this, remove the legs from the tray and put to rest with the breast.

Set the roasting tray on the hob. Pour in the strained cooking juices together with the cider vinegar and 100ml water. Bring to a simmer, scraping up any caramelised juices from the tray using a wooden spoon. Simmer gently for 4–5 minutes. Strain the sauce through a fine sieve and stir in any juices from the rested duck.

Carve the duck, divide among four plates and spoon the sauce over the meat. Serve hot.

● ● ●

Creamed Vanilla Rice Pudding
with Spiced Winter Fruit

Rice pudding is my all-time favourite comfort dessert. As long as it's packed full of vanilla I'm happy to serve it both at home or in my restaurant, and this is a foolproof recipe I've been using for years. The fruit garnish can be changed according to the seasons. I love, equally, both the spices of this winter version and the perfume of wild strawberries in the summer as they hit the warmth of the pudding.

Serves 4

For the rice pudding
200ml milk
300ml double cream
50g caster sugar
1 vanilla pod
100g arborio rice
100ml double cream, whipped

For the spiced winter fruit
60g unsalted butter
150g caster sugar
1 Golden Delicious apple, cored and
   cut into 8 wedges
1 firm Comice pear, cored and cut
   lengthways into 8 wedges
1 vanilla pod, split open lengthways
1 cinnamon stick
2 star anise
2 firm plums, stoned and cut into
   quarters
12 ripe but firm brambles or
   blackberries

Preheat the oven to 150°C (conventional oven 170°C/Gas Mark 3).

Mix together the milk, unwhipped double cream and sugar in a heavy saucepan (preferably one that can also be used in the oven). Split open the vanilla pod lengthways and scrape out the seeds. Add the pod and seeds to the milk and cream. Bring to a simmer.

Add the rice and stir to mix. (Transfer to a baking dish, if necessary). Cover with a buttered piece of greaseproof paper and add a lid, then place in the oven. Cook for 50–60 minutes until the rice is tender, stirring a couple of times during this time to ensure the rice cooks evenly.

Meanwhile, prepare the fruits. Heat a heavy-based frying pan, add the butter and heat until foaming. Add the apple and pear and fry over a medium heat until the fruit is a nice golden brown. Add the sugar, raise the heat slightly and stir until the sugar has melted and caramelised.

Add the split vanilla pod, cinnamon stick and star anise, then pour in 150ml water. Bring to the boil. Add the plums and poach gently until they are tender. Remove from the heat and cool slightly before gently folding in the brambles. Cover and leave to cool to room temperature.

Allow the rice pudding to rest and cool slightly for 10 minutes before folding in the whipped cream. Divide among warmed bowls and serve the winter fruits on the side.

Peter

Gilmore

'Good dark chocolate is my guilty pleasure.'

Gilmore

Harmony is the watchword of one of Australia's most celebrated and recognisable food icons, Peter Gilmore. The executive chef at Sydney's award-winning Quay restaurant is famous for achieving a perfect balance between subtlety of flavour, texture and exquisite presentation in every dish he creates. 'That's the art of the cook.'

It's a far cry from Gilmore's first culinary job of making garlic bread to his fabled snow egg dessert (see his Guava Snow Egg recipe on page 147) but his cuisine is constantly and consciously evolving to echo the cultural diversity of modern Australia, and he is zealous about showcasing and celebrating Australia's natural produce in his cooking, too.

With traditional culinary training in Australia and the UK, it's not surprising that Gilmore uses classical techniques and ingredients in his dishes. But he also likes to expand his food horizons, studying ancient methods of food preservation like fermentation to give him inspiration.

Sydney-born Gilmore's food adventures began in his childhood, sparked and encouraged by his mother. With her advice to 'cook from the heart', he decided on a culinary career at the age of 14, began an apprenticeship in New South Wales aged 16 and spent his twenties working in UK country house hotels – and then London – honing his skills.

Back in Sydney, after spending time in Guillaume Brahimi's kitchen (French-born Brahimi being another celebrated Sydney-based chef) and at De Beers Restaurant at Whale Beach, Sydney, Gilmore finally landed his career-defining post at the Quay in 2001.

Here his skill soon stood out and a clutch of Australian and international awards were showered on him and the Quay. In 2015, a decade-long ambition was fulfilled when he took over the Bennelong Restaurant at Sydney Opera House.

Secret Food Haunt
Victor Churchill butchery, located in Sydney's eastern suburb of Woollahra. Founded in 1876, it's one of Australia's finest and oldest butchers, specialising in quality lamb, pork and beef.

Like most chefs, Gilmore has precious little family time, but when he does manage to hang out with his wife and two sons, they often go out for Chinese tea (yum cha). Nor does the cooking stop just because he's at home: 'I love the buzz of having family around, firing up the pizza oven or making a Thai curry from scratch.'

• • •

Chioggia and Albino Beetroot, Violets, Goat's Curd, Treviso and Wild Cherries

This salad utilises two rarer types of beetroot – Chioggia (candy-striped beetroot) and Albino (pure white beetroot). The combination of these with truffle, sweet violets, bitter Treviso purée, pomegranate molasses crumbs, wild sour cherries and goat's milk curd is an exotic but harmonious range of flavours and textures that play off each other beautifully. The salad builds in intensity on the palate – the flavours move from earthy mellowness to sour, bitter and sharp, and the textures from soft and yielding to crisp, crunchy and creamy. It's a great dish to enliven the palate at the beginning of a meal.

Serves 8

8 baby Chioggia beetroot
8 baby Albino beetroot
8 baby French breakfast radishes
8 golfball-size pink turnips
olive oil
sea salt flakes
100g fresh goat's milk curd

For the pomegranate molasses crumbs

150ml fresh beetroot juice
100ml pomegranate molasses
1½ slices slightly stale sourdough
   bread, 2cm thick, crusts removed
100g clarified butter
100ml grapeseed oil

For the Bull's Blood leaves

20g baby Bull's Blood beetroot leaves
300ml grapeseed oil

For the pickled Treviso purée

100g sugar
100ml balsamic vinegar
400ml grapeseed oil
2 heads Treviso radicchio
100g cooked, peeled beetroot
sea salt and freshly ground black
   pepper

To assemble

extra virgin olive oil
aged balsamic vinegar
50g pitted preserved wild Italian
   cherries
20g fresh or preserved black truffle,
   grated
edible violets, to garnish

To make the pomegranate molasses crumbs, combine the beetroot juice and pomegranate molasses in a small saucepan and boil to reduce by a quarter over a medium heat. Strain into a wide bowl and allow to cool.

Preheat the oven to 100°C (conventional oven 120°C/Gas Mark ½). Add the sourdough slices to the beetroot mixture and soak thoroughly. Transfer the slices to a rack in a roasting tray and dry out in the oven for around 2 hours until the bread is brittle. Break the bread into rough 1cm cubes. Heat the clarified butter with the grapeseed oil in a pan over a medium–high heat and deep-fry the bread until crunchy. Drain on kitchen paper. Cool and store in an airtight container until required.

You can prepare the Bull's Blood beetroot leaves at the same time as the bread is drying out in the oven. Trim half the leaves, then blanch in boiling water for about 10 seconds. Drain and refresh in iced water. Thoroughly dry, then lay the leaves out in a single layer on a lipped baking sheet lined with baking parchment. Place in the oven (with the bread) and allow to dry out for around 20 minutes – watch them carefully, particularly if you have a fan oven, as they're so delicate once dry and may fly about in the oven. Once dry, heat the grapeseed oil in a pan to medium–high and deep-fry the leaves until crisp. Drain on kitchen paper. Keep in an airtight container until needed.

To make the pickled Treviso purée, dissolve the sugar in 100ml water and bring to the boil, then cool. Combine this sugar syrup with the balsamic vinegar and grapeseed oil and pour into a large vacuum-seal bag. Trim off the outer leaves from the Treviso until only the firm heart remains. Cut each heart lengthways in half. Immediately place in the bag of liquid and seal. Steam in a steamer or immerse in a water bath in a sous-vide cooker at 90°C and cook for 20 minutes. Remove from the cooker and allow to cool. (Alternatively, put all the ingredients into a pan with a tight-fitting lid. Bring to the boil, then turn the heat down to its lowest setting and cook very gently until the Treviso is tender when you push a knife into the stalk. Allow to cool).

When completely cold, remove the Treviso hearts, reserving the pickling liquid, and place in a blender with the cooked beetroot. Add 2 tablespoons of the reserved pickling liquid and blitz on high until smooth. Pass the purée through a fine drum sieve. Season and set aside until required.

Now prepare the vegetables. Preheat the oven to 180°C (conventional oven 200°C/Gas Mark 6). Trim the beetroots, radishes and turnips. Put all the beetroots on a large sheet of baking parchment, drizzle over some olive oil and season with sea salt. Wrap into a parcel, then wrap this in foil. Place on a baking tray and bake for 20–25 minutes until just tender. While warm, peel away the skins, then allow to cool a bit.

>

Meanwhile, blanch the baby radishes in boiling salted water for 30 seconds. Drain and refresh in iced water. Peel the pink turnips, then carve them into rough petals. Blanch for 30 seconds; drain and refresh in iced water. Set all the prepared vegetables aside.

Cut the goat's milk curd into small pieces and keep in a cool place.

To assemble, combine the beetroots, radishes and turnips in a mixing bowl and dress with extra virgin olive oil, balsamic vinegar and sea salt. Pipe (or spoon) up to a tablespoon of the Treviso purée into the bottom of each serving bowl. Arrange an equal portion of beetroot, radish and turnip on top of the purée. Scatter pomegranate molasses crumbs, wild cherries and pieces of goat's milk curd over the top. Garnish with fried Bull's Blood leaves, a few of the reserved fresh leaves, grated truffle and fresh violets. Finish with drizzles of balsamic vinegar and extra virgin olive oil.

• • •

Raw Smoked Blackmore Wagyu, Fresh Dory Roe, Horseradish Crème Fraîche and Salty Ice Plant

This dish combines multiple textures and a harmonious contrast of flavours. The salty pop of the dory roe plays off against the intensity of flavour of the Wagyu beef. The horseradish soured cream provides a luscious texture and mouth feel to complete the dish.

Serves 8

For the raw smoked Wagyu beef
1 x 800g centre-cut Wagyu beef rump
  (I get mine from David Blackmore)
150g mixed maple and cherrywood
  chips

For the fresh dory roe
2 litres still mineral water
100g sea salt
400g fresh silver dory roe sacs

For the horseradish crème fraîche
200g horseradish root
150ml crème fraîche
75ml single cream
sea salt

To finish
80ml 10-year-aged traditional Korean
  soy sauce
160ml extra virgin olive oil
finely microplaned zest of 1 lemon
32 small tips of edible ice plant or
  purslane
32 white bean flowers, optional

Cut the beef into four equal portions. Cold-smoke the beef over the wood chips at a constant temperature of 4°C for 1½ hours. To do this, put a small cake ring into a large pan and set a bowl on top, making sure the bowl doesn't come higher than the side of the pan. Pour the woodchips around the outside of the bowl into the pan, then put the beef into the bowl. With the pan lid in one hand and resting close to the top, carefully light the woodchips with a blowtorch. When they're all black and smoking, put the lid on top and leave for the required time. When the beef has finished the cold-smoking process, cover and keep in the fridge.

To prepare the fresh dory roe, divide the water and salt equally between two bowls. Place the fresh dory roe in the first bowl. Using a pair of sharp scissors, cut the skin of each roe sac to expose the roe. Remove the roe from the sac, using a blunt knife to gently scrape it out. Discard the skin. This is a fiddly process, but do persevere as the eggs will release themselves gradually. Using a whisk, gently agitate the eggs to help separate them. Allow the eggs to sit in the salted water for 10 minutes, then carefully pour the eggs on to a fine drum sieve to drain; discard the salted water.

Using a pair of tweezers, remove any veins or blood vessels from the eggs. Carefully transfer the eggs with a palette knife or plastic pastry scraper to the second bowl of salted water. Gently agitate the eggs again using the whisk. Allow to sit for 10 minutes before once more pouring the eggs on to the fine drum sieve. Remove any veins you may have missed the first time, then leave the eggs to drain completely. The yield should be about 300g. Transfer the eggs to a plastic container, seal and keep in the fridge until required.

Peel the horseradish and put through a juicer. Combine the creams with a pinch of salt. To start, mix in half the horseradish juice. Depending on the strength and heat of the horseradish, gradually mix in more juice to taste. The finished cream should be strong but not too overpowering. Keep in the fridge until needed.

To finish, cut the beef into 1cm cubes. Dress with the aged soy and 80ml extra virgin olive oil. Add the remaining 80ml extra virgin olive oil and the lemon zest to the fresh dory roe and gently mix through.

Place 100g of the dressed beef in the centre of each plate and spread out so that the beef is roughly in a single layer. Top with 4–5 teaspoons of the dory roe. Drizzle the horseradish crème fraîche over the dory roe and beef, and garnish with ice plant and bean flowers. Serve immediately.

• • •

Guava Snow Egg

The Snow Egg has become my iconic signature dessert after airing on the finale of MasterChef Australia season 2. The flavours and fruit used can change seasonally. The anticipation of cracking through the toffee-coated egg remains the highlight of this dessert.

Serves 8

For the guava purée
175g caster sugar
½ vanilla pod, split open lengthways
375g strawberry guava flesh

For the guava granita
400g peeled strawberry guavas
100g strawberries
100g caster sugar

For the custard apple ice cream
6 egg yolks
200g caster sugar
200ml milk
1 or more large, extremely ripe custard apples (cherimoyas)
100ml single cream

For the vanilla custard base and vanilla cream
200ml single cream
1 vanilla pod, split open lengthways
1 medium egg
2 medium egg yolks
40g caster sugar
100ml double cream

For the maltose tuiles
200g maltose (maltose syrup)
100g caster sugar
20g flaked almonds
icing sugar, for dusting

For the poached meringues
80g egg whites
80g caster sugar

To make the guava purée, put the sugar and 250ml water in a saucepan. Scrape the seeds from the vanilla pod into the pan and add the pod too. Bring to the boil to dissolve the sugar, then lower the heat to a gentle simmer. Add the guava flesh and simmer for 10 minutes. Remove from the heat and discard the vanilla pod. Drain the guava flesh in a sieve set over a bowl (reserve the cooking liquid), then put the flesh in a blender or food processor and blend until smooth, adding just enough of the cooking liquid to make a thick purée. Pass the purée through a fine sieve. Set aside in the fridge until needed.

Now make the guava granita. Roughly dice the peeled guavas and strawberries. Put the sugar and 500ml water in a large saucepan and bring to the boil, then lower the heat to a slow simmer. Add the diced fruit and gently simmer for 10 minutes. Remove from the heat and allow to infuse at room temperature for 2 hours. Pass the liquid through a muslin-lined sieve into a bowl or jug; discard the solids. Pour the resulting guava syrup into a shallow freezerproof container to a depth of 5cm. Freeze for no less than 12 hours; every 2–3 hours remove from the freezer and scrape with a fork to form the granita crystals. Once the granita is made, it can be kept in the freezer for a day or two.

For the custard apple ice cream, whisk together the egg yolks and sugar in a stainless steel or other heatproof bowl until pale and creamy. Bring the milk just to the boil, then pour on to the egg yolk/sugar mixture while whisking. Set the bowl over a pan of simmering water and whisk for about 10 minutes to make a thick sabayon. Lift the bowl off the pan and set it over ice; leave to cool.

Meanwhile, scoop the flesh from the custard apple into a chinois double-lined with muslin. Gather the muslin at the top and squeeze the ripe custard apple flesh tightly to obtain a clear juice. When you have 300ml of clear juice, whisk it into the sabayon with the single cream. Pour the mixture into an ice cream maker and churn, then transfer the ice cream to a container in the freezer to keep until needed (it can be stored in the freezer for up to 2 weeks).

To make the vanilla custard base, preheat the oven to 150°C (conventional oven 170°C/Gas Mark 3). Pour the single cream into a saucepan. Scrape in the seeds from the vanilla pod and add the pod, too. Heat until the cream just begins to boil, then remove from the heat. Whisk the egg, egg yolks and sugar together in a stainless steel or other heatproof bowl. While whisking, slowly pour on the hot vanilla cream. Remove the vanilla pod. Pour the mixture into a baking dish to a depth of 5cm. Set the dish in a roasting tin of water in the oven and cook for 20–25 minutes until the custard is just set. Remove the dish from the water and cool, then chill the custard for 5–6 hours until fully set.

Next make the maltose discs for the tuiles. Heat the maltose and sugar together in a heavy-based pan until the sugar has dissolved, then boil until the mixture caramelises and reaches the hard crack stage (149–154°C on a sugar thermometer), stirring every now and then to prevent the mixture from burning. Add the flaked almonds and swirl carefully to mix, then immediately pour the mixture on to a silicone mat. Leave to cool completely.

>

Preheat the oven to 180°C (conventional oven 200°C/Gas Mark 6). Break up the now-hard caramel and blitz in a food processor to form a fine powder. To make each disc (you need eight), shake enough of this powder through a coarse sieve on to the silicone mat (placed on a baking sheet) to make a fine layer about 1mm thick. You'll need to do this in batches, depending on how big your baking sheet and silicone mat are. Heat the powder in the oven until it melts and forms a clear liquid praline paste – this takes around 5 minutes. Remove from the oven and, before the praline becomes too hard (1–2 minutes), cut out as many discs as you can using a 15cm metal cutter. Use a palette knife to lift the edge of each one and carefully peel it away from the silicone mat. Repeat until you've made eight discs. Store them interleaved with sheets of baking parchment in an airtight container.

For the poached meringues, you will need a silicone sheet (or two sheets) with 16 x 6cm-wide half-hemisphere moulds. Preheat the oven to 120°C (conventional oven 140°C/Gas Mark 1). Whisk the egg whites in the bowl of a free-standing electric mixer until they form soft peaks. Whisking constantly, slowly add the sugar. Continue whisking until the meringue forms firm peaks.

Spoon the meringue into the moulds and smooth the tops level. Set the silicone sheet in a bain marie or roasting tin of hot water. Place in the oven and cook for 15–20 minutes until the meringues feel just firm to the touch. Remove from the bain marie and allow to cool, then unmould the meringues. Place them on a tray lined with baking parchment and keep in the fridge until needed.

For the vanilla cream, combine 100g of the vanilla custard base with the double cream in a mixing bowl and whisk together until the mixture will form soft peaks. Keep in the fridge until needed.

Just before you are ready to assemble the dessert, make the guava fool. Put 400g of the guava purée in a bowl and gently fold through 200g of the vanilla cream to form a rippled effect.

To finish the snow eggs, take eight of the half-hemisphere poached meringues. Using a teaspoon, remove a small scoop from the centre on the flat side of each half-hemisphere, being careful not to break through the outer edge. Place a small scoop of custard apple ice cream inside the hole you've made. Scoop a small hole in the centre of the flat side of the rest of the half-hemispheres and invert one over each ice cream-filled meringue to form a complete sphere. Place a maltose praline disc on top of each sphere and, using a gentle blowtorch, melt the praline over the sphere. Dust all the spheres with icing sugar.

Put a generous spoonful of guava fool in the bottom of each serving glass. Top the fool with the guava granita, then place a snow egg sphere on top of the granita. Serve immediately.

Peter's tips
• If you can't get hold of custard apple, use 300ml apple juice.
• Any leftover praline can be stored in an airtight container for up to 2 weeks and served sprinkled over ice cream.
• Maltose is available from Asian supermarkets. It's a very thick syrup so dip your spoon in a jug of boiling water to help it slip off easily for weighing.

• • •

Peter
Gordon

'My perfect brekky is Malaysian roti canai.'

Gordon

New Zealand chef-restaurateur Peter Gordon is celebrated in the UK as the king of fusion cuisine. Rightly so. No other chef understands the art of marrying different food cultures better, or practises that art so skilfully or consistently; as he does at his at his award-winning flagship restaurant The Providores and Tapa Room in London.

Like many Kiwis he exudes a relaxed can-do attitude to life and work, which is undoubtedly why he's able to juggle restaurants and consultancies across three continents, write copiously (his own books and for magazines), make frequent appearances at food festivals around the world, keep an eye on his New Zealand vineyard – Waitaki Braids – and raise huge amounts of money for leukaemia research.

Despite all these commitments, Gordon tries to keep a few weekend rituals away from the kitchen. As he's London-based this means Saturday food shopping at the city's Broadway Market and a Sunday jaunt to the Columbia Road flower market. 'It's a routine I've been trying to adopt regularly.'

Other wind-down strategies include swimming, walking and cooking for friends and family; especially a roast leg of lamb, naturally, with 'heaps of veggies and salads'. He likes to have everyone in the kitchen as he cooks, creating a convivial buzz. As you'd expect from someone who 'doesn't get on well with posh', the food is often in the middle of the table in sharing dishes.

Gordon's restaurants, too, always have a friendly, welcoming vibe, be they in London (which, in addition to The Providores is home to his Kopapa eaterie), New Zealand (where his partner and close family still live and where he's put his expertise into Auckland's new Sugar Club and the tapas-influenced Bellotta), or at the two Istanbul restaurants at which he holds consultancies.

It was in his native New Zealand, as the head chef of the original Sugar Club in Wellington, that Gordon initially made his name in 1986 as the first chef to cook Asian influenced food in New Zealand. When the restaurant was moved to London in the late 1990s he repeated its success before moving on to launch The Providores in 2001.

Gordon's cooking abilities are indisputable, but not many people know about another skill: his knack for gardening ('I have green fingers') or the fact that a Kit-Kat is never far from his side!

• • •

Secret Food Haunt

Fin and Flounder, a fishmonger located off Broadway Market, Hackney, East London. It sells responsibly sourced, sustainable wild and farmed fish and shellfish, mainly from the British Isles, but also from further afield. All the usual suspects are sold, plus lesser known flat fish like dab or witch sole. The shop also sells wine, herbs and spices and deli items.

Chunky Vegetable and Borlotti Bean Soup

As the weather cools down in autumn, it's time to start making chunky, comforting soups such as this. Great as a weekend lunch or supper dish when served with toasted, thickly sliced sourdough drizzled with olive oil. Or serve more elegantly as a first course in smaller portions. The sharper the cheese you use to sprinkle over, the better – you need something grunty to cut through the richness of the soup.

Serves 6–8

2 tablespoons olive oil
1 large red onion, sliced
1 tablespoon coarsely chopped herbs
 (rosemary, sage, thyme, oregano)
4 garlic cloves, chopped
½ leek, sliced into 1cm-thick rings,
 washed to remove grit if necessary
2 good pinches of saffron threads (or
 use ½ teaspoon ground turmeric)
200g peeled pumpkin or butternut
 squash flesh, diced
1 parsnip, diced
2 celery sticks, cut into 1cm-thick slices
200g shelled fresh borlotti beans (or
 use 1 x 400g can borlotti beans,
 drained and rinsed)
750ml vegetable or chicken stock
100g green beans, topped and tailed
 and cut into 1cm lengths
¼ broccoli head, cut into chunks
80g cheese (try an aged Cheddar,
 Parmesan, feta or pecorino),
 coarsely grated
salt and freshly ground black pepper
3 tablespoons chives, to garnish

Heat the olive oil in a large saucepan and sauté the onion with the herbs and garlic over a medium heat until caramelised.

Add the leek, saffron, pumpkin, parsnip, celery, borlotti beans and stock. Bring to a simmer, then cover and simmer gently until the pumpkin and parsnip are almost cooked.

Add the green beans and broccoli and cook for a further 10 minutes.

Stir in most of the cheese with salt and pepper to taste. Ladle into piping hot bowls and sprinkle on the chives and remaining cheese.

• • •

Baked Fish and Pine Nuts on Fennel, Chilli and Ginger with Red Rice

*In theory you could make this using any fish, but the thicker the fillet the better
the result, as thin fillets will overcook. Use sustainably sourced fish obviously – I'd
recommend cod, tuna, larger sea bream, hake or monkfish. You can cook the fish on
or off the bone, skin on or off – it's entirely up to you and how fussy your guests are!*

Serves 6

6 x 150g portions of fish (if cooking on
   the bone then allow around 190g per
   portion)
2 fennel bulbs, trimmed and thinly
   sliced crossways
1–2 red or green chillies, chopped
   (don't discard the seeds)
1 fat finger of fresh ginger, peeled and
   julienned or finely grated
3 tablespoons extra virgin olive oil or
   virgin rapeseed oil (the latter will
   give a gorgeous colour)
100g pine nuts
1 tablespoon coarsely shredded
   tarragon or coriander leaves
juice of 2 lemons
salt and freshly ground black pepper

For the red rice
300ml (by volume) basmati rice
4 tablespoons tomato paste
2 spring onions, thinly sliced

Preheat the oven to 180°C (conventional oven 200°C/Gas Mark 6).

Start with the rice. Rinse the rice in a sieve for 10 seconds, then shake well to drain. Tip into a saucepan, add the tomato paste and mix together. Add the spring onions and 600ml cold water. Set the pan over a high heat and bring to the boil, then cover with a tight-fitting lid and turn the heat down so the rice is simmering. Cook for 10 minutes. Remove from the heat and set aside, still covered, in a warm place for at least 15 minutes.

Meanwhile, lay the pieces of fish on a plate, season liberally and bring to room temperature. Heat up a metal roasting dish and sauté the fennel with the chillies and ginger in the oil until wilted, stirring often. Add the pine nuts and cook for another minute, then remove half the mixture from the dish and set aside.

Lay the fish pieces, reasonably close together, on top of the fennel mixture in the dish. Spoon the removed fennel over the fish. Bake in the middle of the oven for 12–15 minutes until the fish is barely cooked.

Remove the dish from the oven. Scatter the tarragon and squeeze the lemon juice over the fish. Serve the fish and fennel on top of small mounds of the rice, with a side salad of baby Gem, cos, rocket and halved cherry tomatoes dressed with a little olive oil and lemon juice.

* * *

Quince Crumble Cake
with Basil Cream

Lovely late-summer quinces go incredibly well with the basil in this recipe, along with the chilli and star anise. It may not be an obvious combination but then it's the unconventional pairing of ingredients that is perhaps my culinary trademark. The crumble brings everything together, texturally, and you can serve this warm or at room temperature.

Serves 8

3 quinces
250g caster sugar
½ red chilli
2 tablespoons grated fresh ginger
3 star anise
¼ vanilla pod, split lengthways
300g plain flour
200g chilled unsalted butter, diced, plus
   another 30g butter for finishing
100g rolled oats

For the basil cream
a loosely packed teacup of basil leaves
   (about 30 leaves)
3 tablespoons caster sugar
100ml thick plain yoghurt
200ml double cream

Peel and quarter the quinces and remove the core. Place in a pot large enough to hold the quinces comfortably and add a quarter of the peels and a quarter of the cores. Rinse the contents of the pan with cold water and drain, then pour in enough fresh cold water to cover by 2cm.

Add half the sugar, the chilli, ginger, star anise and vanilla pod. Bring to the boil, then place a paper cartouche (a large circle of baking parchment with a small hole cut in the middle) on the surface. Cook at a rapid simmer for 2 hours. If the liquid drops too low during this time, top up with boiling water so that the fruit is just covered.

Leave the quinces to cool completely in the liquid – they can be cooked a week in advance and then stored, covered, in the fridge.

Preheat the oven to 170°C (conventional oven 190°C/Gas Mark 5). Line the base and sides of a 24–30cm loose-bottomed cake tin with baking parchment.

Put the remaining sugar, the flour and diced butter in a food processor and pulse-blitz to coarse crumbs. Add the oats and blitz for 5 seconds. Spread half of this crumble mix over the base of the tin.

Drain the quinces (reserve the syrup), then cut each quarter in half and set on top of the crumble in the tin. Spoon the remaining oat mixture over the quinces. Scatter the reserved butter, either melted or cut into small cubes, over the crumble topping. Set the tin on a baking tray and bake for 40–60 minutes until the top is golden and crusty.

Meanwhile, make the basil cream. Pound the basil and sugar together until the basil leaves are crushed (a mortar and pestle works well for this). Mix into the yoghurt, then add the cream and whip to soft peaks.

Leave the cake to cool for 20 minutes before removing it from the tin. Cut into wedges and serve each with a drizzle of the quince poaching liquid and a dollop of basil cream.

• • •

Bill
Granger

'The weekend is a great time to cook for pleasure.'

Granger

T hanks to a vegetarian mother and a father who was a butcher, Bill Granger had a somewhat unusual introduction to food when he was growing up in Melbourne, Australia. However, his parents weren't particularly interested in creative cooking and their son, as he grew up, was left to teach himself the craft of being a chef as his passion for food grew.

His fascination with food blossomed to such an extent that in 1993, aged 24, he dropped out of art school in Sydney to open his first restaurant, bills, in the city's Darlinghurst district. It wasn't long before people were queuing up outside for what became his signature dish of creamy scrambled eggs and ricotta hotcakes. They still do – but interestingly, he himself prefers boiled eggs to their scrambled cousins.

It's been onwards and upwards ever since. Today, Granger is Australia's most recognisable and best-loved food broadcaster and writer; and his infectious, relaxed way of communicating his enthusiasm for cooking has won him fans in the 30-plus countries in which his Australian television series have been shown. He's a very successful international chef-restaurateur, too, with outposts of bills in Japan, Hawaii and South Korea, while in London he has two Granger & Co restaurants.

Since opening in London, Granger and his family (wife Natalie and their three daughters) have based themselves in the British capital, but he spends a large part of his time travelling, promoting books and television series, and looking in on his restaurants. Despite this, now that he

can be, Granger is very strict about taking time off at the weekends. 'It's a great time to cook for pleasure.'

He frequently puts roasts of all kinds on the table ('I like the idea of roasting: the oven does the work for you'), and soups, Thai curries, salads and sprout leaves ('the next kale'), too. And, naturally, there's a ritual to his home-cooking regime: wipe down the benches, put on the music, get a glass of sparkling water or wine in your hand when a dish is 80 per cent done.

Unlike some chefs, creating delicious food at home is obviously a method of relaxation for Granger. In fact, it's a task to get him to leave the kitchen – 'the kids laugh at me because I won't stop cooking!'

• • •

Secret Food Haunt
Provenance Village Butcher, in London's Notting Hill not far from Granger & Co. A modern version of a traditional family butcher, run by a group of New Zealanders, its careful sourcing of meat from around the UK, from both rare and traditional breeds, has earned it an enviable reputation for quality. Wild Scottish venison and New Zealand Wagyu beef is also sold, as is a range of charcuterie and condiments.

Prawn, Fennel and Watermelon Salad with Chilli Dressing

Nothing can wake up your palate and fill you with sunshine quite like an Asian salad. Opposing textures and flavours are what make this salad great. Crunchy raw vegetables, sweet juicy fruit, soft fragrant herbs and sweet prawns are all brought together with a vibrant dressing. Delicious.

Serves 4 as a starter

2 fennel bulbs
650g peeled watermelon flesh, scooped
    with a spoon
a handful of basil leaves
a handful of mint leaves
a handful of coriander leaves
16 raw king prawns, peeled
1 tablespoon light-flavoured oil
sea salt

For the dressing
1 garlic clove, roughly chopped
1 red chilli, chopped
2 teaspoons caster sugar
about 1 tablespoon lime juice
about 1 tablespoon fish sauce
about 1 tablespoon light-flavoured oil

For the dressing, pound the garlic with the chilli and sugar in a pestle and mortar to make a coarse paste. Stir in the lime juice, fish sauce and oil. Taste the dressing and balance the flavours as you wish with more lime juice, fish sauce or sugar. Set aside.

Finely slice the fennel, ideally with a mandoline if you have one. Pile on to a large serving dish with the watermelon and herbs.

Set a large, non-stick frying pan on a high heat. Rub the prawns with the oil and season with sea salt, then place in the hot pan. Cook for 1 minute, then turn and cook for 30 seconds until golden on both sides. Lay the prawns on the salad, drizzle over the dressing and serve immediately.

. . .

Thai Chicken and Sweet Potato Curry

Like most people who cook professionally, I like to eat really spicy foods in my down-time. I guess that after tasting food throughout the day it takes some spice to wake up my tastebuds. And so it is that we eat a lot of curries in my house. I've kept this version of one of my favourites relatively mild, so everyone can add extra chilli at the table, according to taste.

Serves 4

8 skinless, boneless chicken thighs, cut into quarters
2 tablespoons curry powder
1 tablespoon light-flavoured oil
1 red onion, sliced
2 garlic cloves, sliced
3cm piece fresh ginger, grated
2 red chillies, finely chopped
400ml chicken stock
500g sweet potatoes, peeled and cut into chunks
1 stalk lemongrass, crushed with the back of a knife and split
1 tablespoon caster sugar
2 tablespoons fish sauce
250ml coconut milk
a handful of coriander leaves
sea salt

To serve
steamed white rice
lemon wedges
1 red chilli, sliced

Put the chicken and curry powder in a bowl and toss to coat the pieces well. Season with sea salt.

Heat the oil in a large heavy-based pan over a medium heat. Add the chicken and fry for a couple of minutes until looking white and opaque. Add the onion and fry for 2 minutes. Stir in the garlic, ginger and chillies and fry for 1 minute.

Pour in the stock. Add the sweet potatoes, lemongrass, sugar and fish sauce and stir to mix. Pour in the coconut milk. Bring to the boil, then reduce the heat and simmer for 10–15 minutes until the chicken and sweet potatoes are cooked through. Discard the lemongrass.

Scatter the coriander over the curry and serve with steamed white rice, lemon wedges and sliced chilli on the side.

• • •

Sticky Mango Pudding with Coconut Custard

You can't go wrong with this Asian-style version of a sticky toffee pudding. I've also made it with bananas and pineapple and it has been a hit every time. In theory it should serve six, but I've never seen a table of four leave any for later...

Serves 4–6

85g unsalted butter, melted, plus extra
    for greasing
125g plain flour
a pinch of salt
115g caster sugar
2 teaspoons baking powder
250ml milk
1 egg, lightly beaten
1 teaspoon vanilla extract
1 ripe mango, peeled and diced
140g light soft brown sugar
3 tablespoons golden syrup

For the coconut custard
400ml coconut milk
2 egg yolks
3 tablespoons caster sugar
1 teaspoon cornflour

Preheat the oven to 180°C (conventional oven 200°C/Gas Mark 6). Butter a 1.8 litre ovenproof dish and set it on a baking tray.

Put the flour, salt, sugar and baking powder in a bowl. Add the milk, melted butter, egg and vanilla extract and whisk together. Stir in the mango and pour into the baking dish.

Combine the brown sugar, syrup and 250ml boiling water in a small saucepan and bring to the boil; stir to help dissolve the sugar. Pour over the pudding (don't be alarmed by this unusual method; it works beautifully). Bake for 40–45 minutes until golden. Remove from the oven and set aside for 10 minutes before serving.

Meanwhile, put all the ingredients for the custard in a small pan and whisk together. Stir over a low heat, without boiling, for 6–8 minutes until thick enough to coat the back of a wooden spoon. Serve with the pudding.

● ● ●

Angela
Hartnett

'My dream restaurant would be by the sea in Italy.'

Hartnett

Angela Hartnett is one of the brightest female stars in the UK culinary firmament. A former Gordon Ramsay protégé, she has established herself as a formidable chef-restaurateur in her own right, with a number of fine eateries to her name, the most famous being London's Michelin-star Murano.

She is also an MBE (Member of the British Empire), one of the most prestigious public honours in the UK. Not bad for someone who wasn't expected to last two weeks in the tough kitchen that existed at Aubergine, the restaurant that launched Ramsay and many of his then kitchen brigade, on to the London and UK dining scene. That was way back in 1994.

These days, in addition to Murano (which she bought from Ramsay's restaurant group in 2010), she is involved in three other eateries: Hartnett, Holder & Co at the luxury boutique hotel Lime Wood in Hampshire (she is now also a director of the hotel) and Café Murano and Merchants Tavern in London, the latter with her partner, chef Neil Borthwick. Regular television appearances over the last decade and her own food slot in the *Guardian* newspaper have ensured that she has become a familiar face beyond her businesses.

Hartnett's cooking style has strong Italian influences. Her maternal grandparents emigrated from the Bardi area in Northern Italy to Wales and her grandmother, Nonna, was instrumental in inspiring a love of food and cooking in her young grand-daughter. Her mother also passed on recipes – most famously in the family, one for anolini.

She isn't wedded to pasta, though, when she cooks at home. 'Roast chicken one-pot wonders' (see page 176)

are her favoured dishes for family gatherings, while in her professional cooking she fuses Italian influences with a superb French classical technique.

In contrast to her own cooking style, when she eats out she heads for modern British restaurants close to her home in East London: Tramshed and St John Bread & Wine are regular haunts.

But weekends off, when she gets them, are also reserved for catching up on TV shows she's missed – American cult shows like *Curb Your Enthusiasm*, for instance – a packet of plain, salted crisps by her side. 'I'd love to cook dinner for Jerry Seinfeld and Larry David – the funniest men alive!'

• • •

Secret Food Haunt

Jonathan Norris Fishmonger, a London-based fish supplier with shops across the city, in Pimlico, Tufnell Park and Victoria Park as well as a stall in Tachbrook Street market. Fish and shellfish are delivered daily from the West Country and Scotland. Fresh fruit and vegetables are also sold at the shops.

Wild Mushrooms on Toast with Lardo

Yes, it's just mushrooms on toast, but the crème fraîche and, especially, the lardo lift it to new heights. Lardo is pork back fat cured with spices and herbs, usually rosemary. It's cut wafer-thin, and melts gorgeously when you drape it over something hot. Any Italian deli worth its salt should have some. This will serve two to four as a first course, depending on how hungry or greedy you are.

Serves 2–4

4 slices white sourdough
2 garlic cloves, cut in half
30g butter
2 tablespoons olive oil
500g mixed wild mushrooms, brushed or wiped clean (don't wash in water) and sliced or cut in half if large
200ml crème fraîche
2–3 tablespoons chopped flat-leaf parsley
½ lemon, to finish
4 slices lardo
salt and freshly ground black pepper

Chargrill the bread on a hot ridged grill pan until lightly golden on both sides, then rub one side of each slice with half a clove of garlic – the toasted bread will act like a grater, and little bits of garlic and its oil will infiltrate the bread. Set aside.

Heat the butter and olive oil in a frying pan, then fry the mushrooms over a high heat for 3–4 minutes until they start releasing their moisture. Cook for just a minute more, then quickly stir in the crème fraîche and parsley and season to taste. Remove from the heat.

Put two pieces of bread on each plate. Cover with the hot mushrooms, finish with a squeeze of lemon and top with the slices of lardo.

• • •

Pot-roast Chicken, Lemon, Spring Onions and Ginger

This is my version of the classic Italian dish, chicken cacciatore, or hunter's chicken. The ideal one-pot wonder, it can be made with a whole boned chicken, or you can use thighs (as I have here) or drumsticks if you prefer. I like to spice it up slightly and sometimes add a touch of curry powder or paprika. Scoring the chicken skin is essential – this simple process allows the maximum flavour to get into the chicken. It's the perfect dish to put on the stove and leave to cook itself – just turn the heat down and cover with baking parchment. I have added asparagus and spring onions but mushrooms or broccoli could work too.

Serves 4

8 chicken thighs (or a whole chicken, cut into 8 pieces)
good olive oil
a few glugs of white wine (optional)
a squeeze of lemon juice
300g green asparagus, roughly chopped
2 bunches of spring onions, roughly chopped

For the paste
5cm piece of fresh ginger, peeled and chopped
2 garlic cloves
a pinch of red chilli flakes
juice of 1 lemon
salt and freshly ground black pepper

In a pestle and mortar, grind the ginger, garlic, chilli and lemon juice into a paste. Slash the skin and into the flesh of the chicken thighs so they will absorb the flavour, then rub the paste all over them.

Heat a dash of olive oil in a large frying pan. When the oil is hot, put the chicken thighs in, skin side down first, and brown evenly on both sides.

Pour away any excess fat rendered from the chicken skin, then add the white wine and stir to deglaze any caramelised juices on the bottom of the pan. (If you would rather not use wine, you can deglaze with water). Cover with a lid or baking parchment and continue to cook, turning the chicken so it cooks evenly and basting with the juices in the pan, for a further 15–20 minutes until you are able to put a knife straight through the chicken meat.

Add a squeeze of lemon juice, then remove the chicken from the pan and keep warm. Add the asparagus and spring onions to the pan and sauté until just tender. Return the chicken to the pan and mix with the vegetables. Season, then serve immediately.

• • •

Lemon Mousse with Figs

This light, zesty palate-cleanser is an all-round favourite. Whip it up in 15 minutes, then just bung it in the fridge for a couple of hours until you need it. Replace the rich figs with roasted plums if you prefer.

Serves 6

50ml heather honey
6 ripe figs

For the base
70g caster sugar
grated zest of 2 lemons
1 large egg, beaten

For the mousse
3 gelatin leaves
40ml lemon juice
3 egg whites
40g caster sugar
120g low-fat cream cheese
1 tablespoon crème fraîche

Mix together the ingredients for the base in a heatproof bowl. Make a bain marie by setting the bowl over a saucepan of simmering water, then heat the mix, stirring, for a few minutes until it starts to thicken. Allow to cool, then chill in the freezer while you prepare the rest of the ingredients.

Soak the gelatin leaves in a bowl of very cold water to rehydrate, following the instructions on the packet.

When the gelatine is ready, remove it from the water, squeezing out any excess. Gently warm up the lemon juice in a small saucepan, add the gelatine and stir until dissolved. Remove from the heat and set aside.

Next make a Swiss meringue with the egg whites and sugar. Put them in a heatproof bowl and set it over a saucepan of hot water. Simmer for a couple of minutes until the sugar has dissolved and the mix is warm to the touch, then remove from the heat and whisk until the meringue will form stiff peaks and is cool.

Stir together the cream cheese and crème fraîche in a mixing bowl until smooth. Mix in the base from the freezer, then add the gelatine/lemon juice mix and stir well. Lastly, fold in the Swiss meringue. Spoon into ramekins or small glass dishes and leave to set in the fridge for 2–3 hours.

When it's time to serve, put the honey into a pan, add the figs and toss them over a low heat for a couple of minutes until evenly coated. Cut the figs in half and place a couple on top of each mousse.

● ● ●

Tom
Kerridge

'I'm a fan of big pots in the middle of the table for everyone to help themselves.'

Kerridge

om Kerridge could have been an actor gracing British television screens in Agatha Christie whodunits – probably as Thug Number One, or Local Bully ('due to my size!') – but luckily for all those who love the wonderfully tasty, expertly crafted food he serves at his renowned pub, The Hand and Flowers, he quit the small screen and pursued a career as a chef instead.

The Hand and Flowers in Marlow, Buckinghamshire is a multi-award-winning gastro pub, the first two-Michelin-star one in the UK, and it's achieved cult status far beyond English borders. Its international culinary renown has also catapulted Kerridge back on to UK television screens, finding fame initially in the hit show the *Great British Menu* before going on to have three series of his own and front the BBC's long-running *Food and Drink* programme.

Yet despite its success, Kerridge and his wife Beth have resisted pressures to rebrand their pub as a fine-dining restaurant, holding on to its craft beers, good-value wines and convivial atmosphere. And they held off expanding their business interests until 2014 when they opened a second pub, The Coach, also in Marlow.

Kerridge's culinary life began as a young boy, cooking for his younger brother and working mother as he grew up in his home county of Gloucestershire. His mum taught him how to make brown sugar meringues as a child and encouraged his early acting to keep him 'out of trouble!'

Starting his training in Gloucestershire, it wasn't long before he moved eastwards, to fine-dining restaurants in London and Norwich, on his journey to opening the Hand and Flowers. En route he got used to losing weekends to work, but these days he reserves Sundays to spend time with Beth and his three 'mental dogs'.

Cooking for friends and family is an essential part of relaxing too. A glance in his store cupboard would reveal Coleman's English mustard in pride of place, English rapeseed oil and all ingredients necessary for dry meat curing and marinating, while checking out his fridge would probably show a piece of pork or lamb for slow roasting, or perhaps a selection of 'good old English sausages'.

• • •

Secret Food Haunt
Walter Rose & Son, a butcher based in the Wiltshire towns of Devizes and Trowbridge. Specialises in sourcing meat locally from Wiltshire and neighbouring county of Somerset. 'Run by Andy Cook. By God, he knows his meat.'

Brown Crab Mayonnaise
with Whiting Goujons

This simple but very tasty dish, using some of our fantastic British seafood, is full of big flavours and great contrasts of textures. It's really easy to make.

Serves 2–4

3 eggs
150g plain flour
150g panko breadcrumbs
4 skinless whiting fillets, cut into
   goujons (1cm strips)
oil for deep-frying

For the mayonnaise
2 egg yolks
2 teaspoons Dijon mustard
2 tablespoons white wine vinegar
100g brown crab meat
330ml vegetable oil

To serve
salt and freshly ground black pepper

First make the mayonnaise. Put the egg yolks, mustard, white wine vinegar and crab meat in a blender and blend until smooth. With the machine running, slowly pour in the oil through the hole in the lid until the mayonnaise is emulsified. Taste and add seasoning if needed. Keep in a cool place until serving. (This will make more mayonnaise than you need for the dish; any left over can be kept in the fridge for up to 3 days).

Beat the eggs in a bowl. Put the flour in another bowl with some salt and freshly ground black pepper, and the breadcrumbs in a third. Dip the goujons into the flour, then in the egg and finally in the crumbs to coat all over.

Heat oil for deep-frying to 180°C. Deep-fry the goujons in batches until crisp and golden brown on all sides. Drain on kitchen paper, then serve hot with the crab mayo as a dip.

• • •

Duck Egg Sponge with Poached Gooseberries and Lemon Thyme Ice cream

This sums up a 'Great British Pudding' for me: a sponge and gooseberries. Using duck eggs ensures that the sponge is rich and deep in flavour – the gooseberries have a wonderful tartness that cuts through this perfectly. Lemon thyme ice cream gives a herby balance to the dish.

Makes 8

For the lemon thyme ice cream
225ml milk
225ml double cream
100g lemon thyme sprigs
5 egg yolks
25g caster sugar
25g glycerine (optional)

For the butter cream
90g unsalted butter, at room
 temperature
175g icing sugar
about 25ml milk
1 tablespoon lemon thyme leaves
grated zest of 1 large lemon

For the poached gooseberries
about 350g caster sugar
100g lemon thyme sprigs
2 strips of lemon peel
500g small gooseberries, topped and
 tailed

For the meringue
2 egg whites
110g caster sugar
1 tablespoon cornflour
1½ teaspoons white wine vinegar

For the duck egg sponge
135g unsalted butter, at room
 temperature
195g caster sugar
1 duck egg
1 duck egg yolk
160g plain flour
rounded ¼ teaspoon baking powder
90g egg whites (from 3–4 hen's eggs)
grated zest of 1 large lemon

To finish
gooseberry jam
8–16 lemon segments
lemon thyme leaves

Start with the ice cream. Put the milk, cream and half the thyme leaves in a heavy-based saucepan and bring just to the boil. Remove from the heat, cover with clingfilm and leave to infuse for 30 minutes.

Whisk the egg yolks and caster sugar together in a bowl. Bring the milk and cream mix back to the boil, then pass through a sieve on to the yolks while stirring. Pour back into the pan and cook over a low heat, stirring all the time, until the custard reaches 82°C. Pass through a sieve into a bowl and whisk in the glycerine and remaining thyme leaves. Leave to cool down completely.

When cold, pass through a sieve again before churning in an ice cream maker according to the manufacturer's instructions. Keep the ice cream in the freezer.

Meanwhile, make the other components of the dessert. For the butter cream, beat the butter until soft. Gradually sift in the icing sugar and beat into the butter. Mix in enough milk to make a spreadable consistency. Add the lemon thyme and lemon zest. Set aside at room temperature.

To prepare the gooseberries, put the sugar, lemon thyme sprigs and lemon peel in a saucepan and add 500ml water. Bring to the boil, stirring to dissolve the sugar. Tip the gooseberries into a bowl and pour over the lemony sugar syrup (if you like, add more sugar to taste). Cover with clingfilm and leave to poach in the residual heat. Once cool, keep in the fridge.

>

Next, make the meringue. Preheat the oven to 140°C (conventional oven 160°C/ Gas Mark 3). Whisk the egg whites, adding the sugar a tablespoon at a time, until they form stiff peaks. Fold in the cornflour and vinegar. Pipe on to a baking sheet lined with baking parchment in little cone shapes. Dry out in the oven for 7–10 minutes, then turn the oven down to 110°C and continue drying for 8–10 minutes. Set aside to cool.

For the duck egg sponge, turn the oven up to 160°C (conventional oven 180°C/ Gas Mark 4). Grease and line a 20cm springform cake tin.

Cream together the butter and 90g of the sugar in a free-standing electric mixer until very soft and pale. Add the whole duck egg and beat until incorporated, then beat in the duck egg yolk. Sift the flour with the baking powder on to a sheet of greaseproof paper or into a small bowl, then add to the mixer bowl and beat until the flour has been fully incorporated.

Whisk the egg whites with the remaining sugar and the lemon zest to stiff peaks. Fold into the cake mixture in two equal batches. Pour into the tin and bake for 15–25 minutes until the sponge is lightly browned and springs back when gently pressed in the centre. Set the tin on a wire rack. When the sponge is cool, remove it from the tin and peel off the lining paper.

To serve, trim off the crusty edges from the sponge. Spread gooseberry jam over the top, then spread the butter cream on top of the jam (if the buttercream is very soft, place the sponge in the fridge to set the buttercream for a bit).

Using a knife, portion into eight small cakes of whatever shape you like. Top with the drained poached gooseberries and meringue cones. (You can turn any leftover gooseberries into a fool).

Blowtorch the lemon segments until caramelised, then place them on top of the cakes. Sprinkle with lemon thyme leaves. Serve with the ice cream on the side.

• • •

Cherry Clafoutis

Cherry clafoutis is one of the classics, easy to make – almost a dessert version of Yorkshire pudding – and loved by all. The trick to making it is not to overwork the flour and to leave the batter to rest before baking. If cherries aren't your thing, you can always replace them with another fruit of your choice. Figs, pears and apricots are all good, and go very well with the vanilla ice cream.

Serves 4–6

125ml red wine
125g caster sugar
250g stoned cherries

For the vanilla ice cream
250ml milk
250ml double cream
2 vanilla pods, split open
6 egg yolks
85g caster sugar
50ml brandy
15g glycerine (optional)

For the batter
1 egg
2 egg yolks
50g caster sugar
125ml double cream
25ml Kirsch
25g plain flour

To finish
toasted flaked almonds
icing sugar

First make the ice cream. Put the milk, cream and vanilla in a heavy-based saucepan and bring just to the boil. Remove from the heat and leave to infuse for 30 minutes.

Whisk the egg yolks and caster sugar together in a bowl. Pour in the milk and cream mix while stirring. Pour back into the pan and cook over a low heat, stirring all the time, until the custard reaches 82°C. Pass through a sieve into a clean bowl and skim off any froth. Stir in the brandy. Leave to cool down completely, then stir in the glycerine if using. Churn in an ice cream maker according to the manufacturer's instructions, then store the ice cream in the freezer.

Put the red wine and caster sugar in a pan and bring to the boil. Pour over the cherries in a bowl and leave to cool.

To make the batter, whisk the whole egg, yolks and sugar together in a bowl. Add the cream and Kirsch, then fold in the flour just until evenly blended. Set aside to rest for about 20 minutes.

Preheat the oven to 160°C (conventional oven 180°C/Gas Mark 4). Place the drained cherries, in one layer, in a shallow baking dish, or into individual dishes. Pour the batter evenly over the cherries. Bake for 20–25 minutes until puffed up, like a low-risen Yorkshire pudding, and golden.

Scatter toasted flaked almonds and sifted icing sugar over the clafoutis before serving – it's best served warm but good at room temperature too.

• • •

Tom
Kitchin

'I always treasure an opportunity to enjoy a meal and a chat with my wife.'

Kitchin

In Scotland's capital city, Edinburgh, there's a magnet for serious food aficionados created by a chef with a cherubic face and riotous hair: The Kitchin restaurant. It's the domain of the appropriately named Tom Kitchin, whose gutsy, seasonal cooking – which he dubs 'from nature to plate' – has won fans from all over the UK and beyond.

His cooking celebrates his local Scottish ingredients ('I've a wealth of amazing produce right on my doorstep – it's every chef's dream!') and is in essence what the French call terroir cooking. In fact, it's the classical techniques of French cuisine that have formed him, taught to him by a trio of legendary French chefs: Guy Savoy, Alain Ducasse and the London-based Pierre Koffmann, with whom he worked for five years and whose book on Gascon cooking still has pride of place on his kitchen bookshelf.

Kitchin's first steps toward a culinary life began aged 13 washing pans in a local pub in Kinnesswood, Scotland where he grew up. He 'loved the thrill' of being in a busy, working kitchen and three years later signed up for catering college armed with a piece of advice from his mother: 'always put a dash of Lea & Perrins [Worcestershire sauce] in your mince and tatties!'

Just over a decade later, in 2006, he and his Swedish wife Michaela opened The Kitchin and within seven months his cooking gained a prestigious Michelin star for the restaurant. Many awards followed, plus two new eateries in Edinburgh (both joint ventures with fellow chef Dominic Jack) – another restaurant, Castle Terrace (awarded a Michelin star in 2012), and a gastropub, The Scran & Scallie.

The gastropub gave Kitchin the chance to revive, with a modern twist, traditional British comfort dishes, the sort he's more likely to cook at home on a Sunday for Michaela and their four young sons. 'Roast with all the trimmings, placed in the middle of the table for everyone to feast on', for instance, which might follow his favoured Sunday breakfast of smoked haddock and a poached egg.

And if he has a hunger pang between meals, well Kitchin's snacking runs to guilty pleasures like chip butties, or more wholesome delights such as crispy ox tongue sandwiches which are 'always a winner at home'.

• • •

Secret Food Haunt
I. J. Mellis, an Edinburgh cheesemonger established originally in the city's Victoria Street in 1993. It specialises in European and British artisan and farmhouse cheeses and there are now three shops in Edinburgh, one in Aberdeen and one in Glasgow. The feel is traditional, but the storage and cheese maturing facilities are hi-tech making the cheeses sold some of the finest in Scotland.

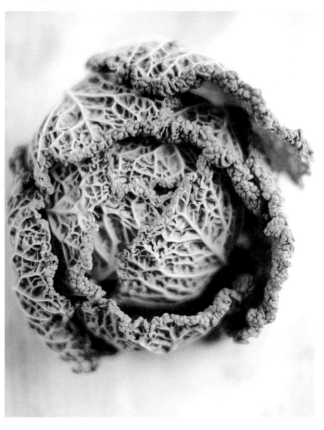

Scotch Broth

For me, no traditional Scottish meal is complete without a hearty Scotch broth.
Usually it's made with lamb, but I like to give it a twist by adding mutton to mine:
it creates a truly juicy depth of flavour.

Serves 6

100g pearl barley
75g dried split peas
1 x 1kg piece of mutton shoulder, flank
  or neck (bone in)
1 teaspoon salt
1 large onion, chopped
1 large leek, chopped
3 carrots, peeled and diced
¼ small Savoy cabbage, shredded
1 medium swede, diced
2 celery sticks, diced
2 garlic cloves, crushed
1 tablespoon chopped parsley
salt and freshly ground black pepper

Soak the pearl barley and the split peas in separate bowls of cold water for a minimum of 3 hours, preferably overnight. Drain and rinse well.

Trim excess fat from the piece of mutton. Put the mutton and pearl barley in a pot with 2 litres cold water and slowly bring to a simmer. Add the salt. Cover and simmer for 45 minutes, occasionally skimming off any fat or residue that floats to the surface.

Add the vegetables, garlic and split peas and continue to simmer gently for up to an hour until the mutton is thoroughly cooked. Add a little water if the broth is looking too dry.

Remove the mutton from the pot and separate the meat from the bone. Tear the meat into shreds and return to the pot. Season to taste with salt and black pepper. Serve hot, sprinkled with parsley.

• • •

Herring with Swedish Sauce and Potato Salad

Herring is something my wife Michaela has grown up eating and enjoying in her native Sweden. This delicious Swedish sauce recipe is one that was used by her grandfather, Sven.

Serves 4

4 herrings
3 carrots, peeled and sliced into thin rounds
2 shallots, thinly sliced
1 star anise
10 black peppercorns
1 tablespoon salt
1 garlic clove, crushed
1 red onion, cut into 3mm-thick strips
125ml white wine vinegar
a handful of chopped spring onions, to garnish

For the bouquet garni
2 leek leaves
a handful of parsley sprigs
a handful of thyme sprigs
1 bay leaf

For the potato salad
600g baby new potatoes
1 red onion, sliced
olive oil to drizzle

For the Swedish sauce
3 tablespoons Dijon mustard
2 tablespoons clear honey
1 tablespoon caster sugar
½ teaspoon salt
1 tablespoon white wine vinegar
200ml vegetable oil
a handful of chopped dill

sea salt and freshly ground black pepper

First prepare the soused herrings. Clean and gut the herrings; remove the pin bones, then fillet the fish (or ask your fishmonger to do all of this for you). Set aside.

To make the bouquet garni, lay one leek leaf flat on a board, put the herb sprigs on top and cover with the other leek leaf; tie with kitchen string to secure. Put the bouquet garni, carrots, shallots, star anise, peppercorns, salt and garlic in a pan with 1 litre cold water and bring to the boil. Cover and simmer for 15 minutes. Add the red onion and white wine vinegar and simmer for another 15 minutes. Remove from the heat and leave to infuse for 10 minutes.

Gently roll up each herring fillet and secure with a wooden toothpick or skewer. Add the herrings to the stock, which should now be nearly at room temperature. Bring back to a simmer and poach the fish gently for 10 minutes, taking care not to let the liquid bubble. Leave the herrings to cool in their marinade, then refrigerate, still in the marinade, overnight.

Next make the potato salad. Cook the baby potatoes in boiling salted water for 12–15 minutes until just tender; drain and thickly slice them. Put the potatoes into a large bowl with the red onion. Season with sea salt and pepper to taste and drizzle over a little olive oil. Toss gently to mix. Set aside in a cool place.

To make the Swedish sauce, mix together the mustard, honey, sugar, salt, a pinch of black pepper and the vinegar. While whisking (an electric mixer is ideal for this), add the oil drop by drop, or pour it in very slowly, until the sauce thickens. Add some of the chopped dill plus an extra sprinkle of black pepper for added flavour.

To serve, take the herrings, still rolled, from the marinade and place on the plates. Add the carrots and pickled red onion from the marinade. Garnish with the rest of the chopped dill and the spring onions. Cover generously with the Swedish sauce and serve with the potato salad.

• • •

Artichoke Barigoule with Chorizo

This is a phenomenal light supper, easy to prepare in advance, quick to cook and incredibly tasty. Its secret lies in the timing; have all the ingredients prepared in advance so they can be added at the right moment, without delay.

Serves 4

juice of 2 lemons (kept seperately)
6 large globe artichokes
olive oil for cooking
250g good-quality chorizo sausages, diced
4 carrots, peeled and sliced
4 shallots, sliced
2 garlic cloves, chopped
1 teaspoon coriander seeds
250ml white wine
1 tablespoon chopped parsley

For the chicken stock

2kg raw chicken carcasses
½ leek (white part), roughly chopped
½ white onion, roughly chopped
2 sprigs of thyme
1 bay leaf
5 white peppercorns

For the bouquet garni

2 leek leaves
a handful of parsley sprigs
a handful of thyme sprigs
1 bay leaf

sea salt and freshly ground black pepper

First make the chicken stock. Remove any excess fat from the chicken carcasses and roughly chop them up. Place in a large saucepan and pour on 3.5 litres cold water to cover. Bring to the boil, then lower the heat and simmer gently for 20 minutes, skimming frequently to remove impurities that float to the surface. Add the chopped vegetables, herbs, peppercorns and a little salt. Simmer gently for a further 1½ hours.

Pass the stock through a fine sieve into a bowl; allow to cool, then keep in the fridge until required. Remove any fat from the surface before using. (This stock can be kept in the fridge for 3–4 days or frozen for 3–4 months).

To prepare the artichokes, fill a large bowl with cold water and add the juice of 1 lemon. Using a small knife, cut off the outer leaves from the artichokes, then carefully peel away the outer skin from the artichoke hearts and stalks. Cut the artichoke hearts into wedges, with stalk. Scoop out the feathery choke in each wedge. As soon as each artichoke is prepared, immerse in the lemon water to prevent browning.

Heat a heavy-based frying pan or sauté pan (with a lid). Add a drizzle of olive oil, then the chorizo sausages and cook, stirring, for 2–3 minutes to release their oil.

Remove the artichokes from the lemon water and pat dry on kitchen paper. Add them to the pan, put the lid on and sweat gently for 2–3 minutes.

Meanwhile, to make the bouquet garni, lay one leek leaf flat on a board, put the herbs sprigs on top and cover with the other leek leaf; tie with kitchen string to secure. Add to the pan along with the carrots, shallots, garlic, coriander seeds and remaining lemon juice. Cover the pan again and sweat for 2–3 minutes, stirring occasionally; this will release a lot of flavour.

Pour in the white wine and boil to reduce right down until dry. Measure out 500ml stock. Ladle in enough of the stock to just cover the ingredients and simmer, uncovered, for 15 minutes until all the vegetables are cooked, adding more stock as it reduces.

Check the seasoning, adding salt and pepper to taste. Remove the bouquet garni and scatter over the chopped parsley before serving.

• • •

Atul
Kochhar

'Outside my work, I'm still a cook.'

Kochhar

A trail-blazer for an elegant Anglo-Indian cuisine, Atul Kochhar has been instrumental in changing the perception of Indian food through his London restaurant Benares and, more recently, as his restaurant empire has expanded, in Ireland and the Middle East.

Drawing on his Indian culinary heritage with all its history of spicing expertise, but cooking with top British produce, he's fused the food of his birth-country and his adopted country seamlessly: a skill recognised by both the highly respected Michelin guide when it awarded Benares a Michelin star in 2007 and by a wider television audience after Kochhar's appearances on the influential show *Great British Menu* and, subsequently, his own TV series.

With strong culinary influences from both his parents, Kochhar's food education began early in eastern India where he was born. Like many great Indian chefs he learned his trade, though, with the Oberoi hotel group – and also in the kitchen of the India-based German chef Bernhard Koenig.

Travelling to England to head up the Indian restaurant, Tamarind, in London in 1994, he found that though Indian food was hugely popular in the UK it was definitely not fine-dining. He soon put that to rights, winning the restaurant a Michelin star in 2001 before launching Benares in 2003 and repeating the accolade for his own restaurant. His restaurant kingdom now includes two more UK restaurants, a Dublin venture and one in Dubai.

In between running his businesses and writing books, Kochhar likes to feed his family at home. As with many chefs, cooking away from their restaurants takes an altogether more traditional and simpler form and he often thumbs through his father's collection of recipes, or his wife Deepti's diary in which she writes down her own ideas for dishes.

He also rates his mother's recipe for turnips, Punjabi style. Garam masala is always to hand as are the often under-rated lentils ('full of nutrition').

Kochhar isn't entirely Indian in his eating habits, though. He also likes to indulge in a 'good cheese sandwich', or chocolate – but only to calm him down when he's angry!

• • •

Secret Food Haunt
Osterley Park Farm Shop, in Isleworth, West London. Part of the National Trust's property portfolio – one of the last surviving country estates in Greater London – the shop sells vegetables and eggs grown and produced on site.

Salmon Brochettes Marinated in Mustard and Honey

Salmon has a lovely texture, and its brilliant flavour prompts cooks to create some great combinations. I have used really easy spicing here to let the salmon do the talking.

Serves 4 as a starter

400g salmon fillet, skinned and cut into 3cm cubes
1 red and 1 green pepper, cut into 3cm squares
1 red onion, cut into 3cm squares
30g butter, melted
1 tablespoon finely chopped coriander leaves
1 teaspoon chaat masala
1 lemon, cut into wedges

For the ginger-garlic paste
100g garlic, chopped
100g fresh ginger, peeled and chopped
2 tablespoons vegetable oil (if you're not using the paste straight away)
1 tablespoon lemon juice (if you're not using the paste straight away)

For the onion raita
200g Greek-style yoghurt
½ teaspoon cumin seeds, toasted in a dry frying pan
a pinch of crushed black pepper
½ teaspoon lime juice (optional)
2–3 tablespoons finely chopped red onion

For the tikka marinade
250g Greek-style yoghurt
1 tablespoon ginger-garlic Paste (see above)
1 tablespoon lemon juice
1 tablespoon Dijon mustard
1 tablespoon honey
1 tablespoon ajwain seeds
1 teaspoon black peppercorns, coarsely crushed
1 teaspoon ground coriander
½ teaspoon red chilli powder
½ teaspoon garam masala

½ teaspoon ground turmeric, or a few strands of saffron
1 tablespoon finely chopped fresh ginger
1 tablespoon tomato paste (optional)
sea salt

First make the ginger-garlic paste. Blend the peeled garlic and fresh ginger with 100ml water, using a blender or mini food processor. Keep in a sealed container in the fridge. If you want to keep the paste for longer than a few days, add the oil and lemon juice when you blend. Then it will keep for up to one week. Or you can freeze the paste in ice-cube trays.

Next make the raita. Whisk all the ingredients together and keep in the fridge until required.

Mix all the ingredients for the marinade together with sea salt to taste and set aside in a non-metallic container in the fridge for 20 minutes. Add the fish, peppers and onion to the marinade and leave in the fridge for 1–2 hours.

Thread 2–3 pieces of fish each on four metal skewers (or wooden ones that have been soaked in cold water for an hour), alternating the fish with the peppers and onion. Heat a well-oiled ridged grill pan, or prepare a barbecue. Add the fish and cook for about 12 minutes on each side until lightly coloured. The fish should be firm and opaque when cooked. Brush with the melted butter, then sprinkle with the chopped coriander and chaat masala. Serve with the raita and lemon wedges on the side.

• • •

Chicken Liver Curry

This curry can be served as a main course with rice or as a snack with drinks, either placed neatly on small pieces of crisp naan bread or simply with a few toothpicks.

Serves 4

2 tablespoons vegetable oil
1 tablespoon finely chopped garlic
1 tablespoon finely chopped fresh
  ginger
2 onions, finely chopped
1 tablespoon ground coriander
2 teaspoons ground cumin
½ teaspoon ground turmeric
1 teaspoon red chilli powder
600g chicken livers, cleaned and diced
1 mango, peeled and diced
2 tomatoes, diced
2 tablespoons finely chopped coriander
  leaves
sea salt

Heat the oil in a pan and sauté the garlic, ginger and onions together until lightly coloured. Add all the ground spices and sauté for a minute, then add the chicken livers and stir to coat them well with the spices. Cook, stirring, for 3–4 minutes until the livers have lost their raw look. Add the mango, tomatoes and sea salt to taste and cook gently for 2–3 minutes until the livers are cooked through. Serve hot, sprinkled with chopped coriander.

• • •

Stack of Atul's Doughnuts, Pomegranate and Rose Frozen Yoghurt

Doughnuts are sin food but they are a must! I love them a lot and just to reduce the guilt I have added lots of fruits to this recipe. I love it and I know my guests at Benares love it and I hope you all will love it too!

Serves 4–6

For the frozen pomegranate, Turkish delight and rose yoghurt
70g pomegranate juice
100g condensed milk
250g thick Greek yoghurt
40g Turkish delight, chopped
1 teaspoon rose water

For the doughnut dough
500g strong plain flour
2g salt
50g caster sugar
100g unsalted butter
15g fresh yeast or 7g fast-action dried yeast
250ml lukewarm milk (no more than blood temperature, 32°C)
oil for deep-frying

For the raspberry and rose coulis
300g fresh raspberries
250g caster sugar
rose water

For the curry syrup
25g toasted cumin seeds
25g toasted coriander seeds
2–5g ground turmeric
Maldon sea salt to taste
500g caster sugar
500ml water

For the doughnut glaze
200g icing sugar
toasted coriander seeds
toasted cumin seeds

To garnish
rose petals
pomegranate seeds

Make the frozen yoghurt the day before. Put all the ingredients in a food processor and blitz until smooth, then chill well. Transfer to an ice cream maker and churn until softly set. Spoon into a freezerproof container, cover and freeze until firm. Keep in the freezer until 10–15 minutes before serving.

To make the doughnut dough, sift the flour, salt and sugar into a bowl. Rub in the butter to make a fine breadcrumb texture. If using fresh yeast, mix it with the warm milk, then pour into the flour mixture. If using dried yeast, stir it into the flour mixture, then add the warm milk. Bring together to make a soft but firm, unsticky dough.

Turn out on to a lightly floured surface and knead for about 2 minutes until smooth. Cover the dough with a cloth or clingfilm and leave to rise in a warm place until doubled in size.

Knock back the dough to deflate it. Roll out on a floured surface to about 1.5cm thickness. With a 5cm plain cutter, stamp out rounds. Use a smaller cutter to make a central hole in each round. Place the shaped doughnuts on a tray lined with baking parchment and leave to prove in a warm place until doubled in size. The shaped doughnuts can be kept in the freezer on the lined tray, then proved and cooked from frozen.

Meanwhile, make the coulis and the curry syrup. For the raspberry and rose coulis, put the raspberries and sugar in a pan with 2 tablespoons water and bring to the boil, stirring to dissolve the sugar. Pour into a blender or food processor and blitz to a purée, then strain through a fine sieve. When cold, add a few drops of rose water to the coulis to flavour it. Do not make it overpowering. Set aside.

For the curry syrup, grind all the spices and salt together to a powder. Tip into a saucepan and add the sugar and water. Bring to the boil, stirring to dissolve the sugar. Pass through a fine chinois into a baking tray. Set aside.

Preheat the oven to 100°C (conventional oven 120°C/Gas Mark ½).

Heat a pan of oil (or oil in a deep-fat fryer) to 170°C. Deep-fry the doughnuts, in small batches, until they are golden on both sides. As the doughnuts are fried, immediately drop them into the curry syrup. Leave the doughnuts to soak for 5 minutes until swollen. Lift them out of the syrup and leave to cool.

To make the doughnut glaze, sift the icing sugar into a bowl and stir in enough of the curry syrup to make a translucent glaze the thickness of thick glacé icing. Dip the doughnuts one by one into the glaze to give them a fine coating all over and place on a baking tray lined with baking parchment. Sprinkle half of the doughnuts with toasted coriander seeds and the other half with toasted cumin seeds.

Place the tray of doughnuts in the oven for about 1 minute just to set the glaze. (Don't let the glaze get too hot or it will blister and will no longer be smooth).

Serve the doughnuts warm with the frozen yoghurt and coulis, garnished with rose petals and pomegranate seeds.

• • •

Pierre
Koffmann

'My grandmother, Camille, is my culinary hero.'

Koffmann

It was international rugby union that lured one of London's most famous adopted culinary sons, Frenchman Pierre Koffmann, to British soil in 1970. Having played the sport for Toulon back home (picking up a dodgy knee in the process), he wanted to see France challenge England at the home of English rugby, Twickenham. He expected to stay in the UK for six months at most, but months turned into years and he never went back.

In the UK, Koffmann's reputation as a chef is unparalleled. His three-Michelin-star London restaurant La Tante Claire (closed over a decade ago, when he wanted to take a break from cooking) remains the stuff of legend, and his current restaurant – Koffmann's, at London's Berkeley hotel – is always buzzing. He has trained and influenced some of the biggest names on the UK dining scene: among them Gordon Ramsay, Jason Atherton and Tom Kitchin.

Born in Tarbes, Gascony, Koffmann absorbed a love and knowledge of food from his mother and maternal grandmother. Watching his grandmother, Camille, cook over an open fire in her farmhouse using produce from the surrounding land was particularly inspiring for him. In his own cooking he has always spotlighted the food traditions of Gascony and is famous for using every last bit of any produce he cooks with.

Surprisingly, Koffmann fell into cookery school at the age of 15 (he tried a number of other trades first). He then worked in France and Switzerland before crossing the English Channel to London, aged 22. Once there, he worked for the godfathers of British cuisine – the Roux brothers – before eventually opening La Tante Claire in 2003.

It's his remarkable ability to extract flavour from any ingredient that diners crave – pig's trotters are just one example. Customers still clamour for his signature dish of pig's trotters with chicken mousseline, sweetbreads and morels, originally on the menu at La Tante Claire.

Nicknamed 'the bear' by his cheffing colleagues, Koffmann does little cooking at home these days, preferring to leave the kitchen to wife, Claire, whose roast pork he says, is 'the best'. There's little doubt, though, that he's passed on his mother's tip to 'always cook for two extra people' – just in case of unexpected visitors.

• • •

Secret Food Haunt
Clifton Greens, a greengrocer in London's Maida Vale district. Known for the wide variety and 'brilliant' quality of fruit and vegetables that it sells.

Shoulder of Lamb
with Potatoes

*This is one of our Sunday lunch favourites, straight from
my boyhood in France where the tradition is to give the
dish to the baker to cook in the village oven.*

Serves 6

1 x 1.8kg shoulder of lamb (bone in)
6 garlic cloves, slivered
150g duck fat
2 large onions, sliced
700g potatoes (not too floury), peeled
  and thinly sliced
2 teaspoons chopped thyme
salt and freshly ground black pepper

Preheat the oven to 180°C (conventional oven 200°C/Gas Mark 6).

Season the lamb all over. Make little slits in the meat and insert the slivers of garlic. Heat 100g of the duck fat in a roasting tin and put in the lamb. Roast for 40 minutes, basting frequently with the fat in the tin.

Meanwhile, fry the onions in the remaining duck fat until golden brown.

Remove the roasting tin from the oven and lift out the lamb. Make a layer of half of the potato slices over the base of the tin. Spread the onions on top, then make a second layer of potatoes. Add 100ml water and sprinkle the thyme over the potatoes. Set the lamb on top.

Return to the oven and roast for 35 minutes until the potatoes are cooked, basting the meat and potatoes with the juices in the tin from time to time. Season to taste before serving.

• • •

Madeleines

*We always have Madeleines when we have friends over. We put
a bowl of them on the table and serve them with a liqueur plus, in
the autumn, wet walnuts and chestnuts.*

**Makes 12 large or
24 mini madeleines**

melted butter and plain flour for the
  tray
2 eggs
100g caster sugar
100g plain flour
¾ teaspoon baking powder
½ teaspoon orange flower water
100g unsalted butter, melted

Preheat the oven to 180°C (conventional oven 200°C/Gas Mark 6). Brush a madeleine tray with melted butter, then shake in a little flour to coat; tap to remove the excess flour.

Whisk together the eggs and sugar in a bowl until frothy. Lightly whisk in the remaining ingredients.

Spoon into the shell-shaped cups in the tray. Bake for 8–10 minutes until the madeleines have risen a little in the middle and are firm to the touch. Transfer the madeleines to a wire rack and leave to cool for a few minutes before serving.

• • •

Summer Fruits
in Red Wine

This is one of our family favourites and a super fast dish to prepare if you're time starved. The fruit works beautifully with the red wine. When I was a kid it was always a great treat when my grandmother made it because I got to taste some wine!

Serves 4

1 litre red wine
½ cinnamon stick
10 black peppercorns
150g caster sugar
100g stoned cherries
100g blueberries
100g raspberries
100g strawberries

Combine the wine, cinnamon stick, peppercorns and sugar in a saucepan. Bring to the boil, stirring to help dissolve the sugar, then boil for 3 minutes.

Remove from the heat and add the cherries to the pan. Leave to cool.

When the spiced syrup is cold remove the cinnamon stick. Add the remaining fruit and leave to macerate for 2 hours. Serve lightly chilled.

• • •

Jamie
Oliver

'My dream restaurant would be in the middle of a giant vegetable patch in Regent's Park, London.'

Oliver

Chef, restaurateur, television phenomenon, author: Jamie Oliver has achieved so much since he shot to fame with his first UK television series in 1999 that he is now one of the most influential operators within the British restaurant industry. Indeed his popularity and influence has spread via books and TV shows to over 100 countries around the world.

With a huge empire of over 40 restaurants (including the London barbecue steakhouse Barbecoa and an international high-street collection of Jamie's Italian restaurants), 30 TV series (many of them successfully campaigning for better eating habits at home and in schools on both sides of the Atlantic) and a clutch of cookbooks to his name, this Italian-inspired culinary guru has garnered countless accolades. Perhaps the most prestigious is being made an MBE (Member of the British Empire) which he received in 2003, one of the UK's most important public honours.

Oliver's own culinary journey began in the kitchen of his parents' pub, The Cricketers, in Clavering, Essex. Prepping vegetables from the age of eight he developed a natural appreciation of rustic home-cooked food, which served him well when he found himself in the kitchen of London's River Café with its emphasis on uncluttered, artisanal Italian ingredients.

His charismatic charm got him noticed when a film documentary crew visited the River Café, after which he landed a TV series of his own, *The Naked Chef*. It was a hit and Oliver has never since rested on his laurels, often using his public profile to good effect, be it for lobbying politicians to improve food standards or, famously, to set up the Fifteen restaurant project to train young adults from disadvantaged backgrounds as chefs and front-of-house staff in its three locations.

Despite his mega-busy career, Oliver has never lost sight of his family roots, often reviving comforting childhood dishes for his fans; his mum's retro trifle – 'an esteemed dessert' – has even trended on Twitter. And his wife, Jools, and their four children pop up naturally in his TV programmes.

He eats at home as he cooks on television and his trademark enthusiasm for all things edible is always finding new produce to champion. Celery, for example: 'It's amazing cooked, raw, shaved, grated, chopped, whole and stuffed with beautiful things; or braised with tomatoes, red wine and herbs.'

• • •

Secret Food Haunt

Crystal Waters Traditional Smokehouse is owned and run by the Eastwood family (including 'Dan the Man – my mobile fishmonger'). Based in Lowestoft, Suffolk, it has five smokehouses and also trades fresh fish. Smoked specialities are kippers, haddock and hot-smoked salmon. It supplies many fish stalls in East England, including ones in Southwold, Saffron Waldon and Newmarket.

Delicious Tarragon Salad with
Sweet Grapes, Salted Ricotta and Shaved Walnuts

We eat salads every day at home – enjoying them as a meal in their own right for lunch, as a side with every meal, or even as a kind of leafy, deconstructed-kinda salsa. This beauty of a salad is very unusual because it really heroes the herb tarragon, using it generously, just like you'd normally use rocket. Paired simply with different-coloured grapes, salted ricotta and a delicate dressing, then finished with shavings of walnuts, this becomes a really unique treat. Whether served with roast chicken, seared steaks or cured meats, it's a real joy.

Serves 4

2 banana shallots
4 tablespoons red wine vinegar
2 large bunches of tarragon
1 bunch of red grapes
1 bunch of green grapes
2 tablespoons Dijon mustard
6 tablespoons extra virgin olive oil
2 swigs of Barolo or good red wine
  (optional)
75g hard salted ricotta
a handful of walnuts
sea salt and freshly ground white
  pepper

Very finely slice the shallots, ideally on a mandoline (use the guard!) and put them in a small bowl with a good pinch of sea salt. Cover with the vinegar, making sure the shallots are completely submerged, and leave for 5 minutes to make a quick pickle.

Meanwhile, pick the tarragon leaves into iced water, then drain, spin dry and put into a salad bowl. Finely slice, halve or leave the grapes whole (depending on their size), removing the seeds, if needed, and add to the bowl. Remove the shallots from the vinegar (save this) and scatter them over the grapes.

Put the mustard, oil, Barolo (if using) and 2 tablespoons of the reserved pickling vinegar into a jam jar along with a good pinch of sea salt and white pepper. Pop the lid on and give it a good shake until you have a beautifully glossy, creamy-looking dressing. Pour most of the dressing over the salad and gently toss together, then use tongs to divide the salad among four plates.

Use your mandoline (or use a speed-peeler or box grater) to shave ricotta over each portion, then carefully shave over the walnuts. Drizzle over some of the reserved dressing (any leftovers can be kept for another day) and tuck in right away.

. . .

Tonno di Nonna Fangitta
(Poached Tuna with Sicilian Tomato Sauce)

I first saw this incredible dish when I travelled around the island of Sicily, where it was served with couscous because of the Arabic influence on the local cuisine. Since then, I've evolved it into an absolute family favourite by turning it into a pasta dish, which everyone seems to love. Served with a lemony-dressed green salad on the side, it makes the perfect dinner.

Serves 4–6

400g MSC-approved yellowfin or
   skipjack tuna fillet
1kg ripe mixed-colour tomatoes
3 garlic cloves
1 red chilli
2 sprigs of rosemary
olive oil
4 anchovy fillets
1 heaped teaspoon dried oregano
1 cinnamon stick
a small handful of capers, rinsed
2 x 400g cans good-quality plum
   tomatoes
320–480g wholewheat spaghetti
½ bunch of basil
sea salt and freshly ground black
   pepper

Firstly, you need a pot that your tuna will fit into snugly, so that it poaches completely submerged. Putting the tuna aside, place the pot on a high heat and fill with boiling water from the kettle. Plunge in the fresh tomatoes and leave for just 40 seconds, then drain in a colander and place into a bowl of cold water to cool. Peel off the skins, then remove the seeds and cores and very roughly chop the flesh.

Use a sharp knife to stab eight holes into the tuna at an angle. Finely slice the garlic with the chilli. Stuff one slice of garlic, one slice of chilli and a pinch of rosemary leaves into each incision.

Return the empty pot to a medium heat and add a little oil, along with the remaining garlic, chilli and rosemary leaves, and the anchovies, oregano, cinnamon and capers. Slowly fry until lightly golden. Add the fresh and canned tomatoes, breaking them up with a wooden spoon (I tend to use my hands). Bring to the boil, then reduce to a gentle simmer and cook for 10 minutes.

Season the sauce well, then carefully add the tuna, pushing it down until completely submerged. Put the lid on, slightly ajar, and simmer very gently for 25 minutes (depending on the thickness of your tuna). You'll know it's cooked through when you can easily flake it apart. Remove from the heat, discard the cinnamon stick and check the seasoning.

Cook the pasta in a large pan of salted boiling water, according to packet instructions. When the pasta is almost ready, flake the tuna apart. Drain the spaghetti and toss with the tuna and sauce in the hot pan. Pick the basil leaves and tear over the pasta, then serve.

The leftovers (if there are any) are delicious on toasted bruschetta with a cheeky fried egg on top.

• • •

Jools' Big Fat Birthday Cake
(Chocolate, Cappuccino, Praline and Love)

When you've got something to celebrate, it's important to do it in style, and this is the cake I made for Jools recently as she's just celebrated a 'special birthday'. Now, my missus is pretty incredible, so I wanted a cake that totally delivered. This one is all about the layers and it's dressed to impress. Of course I've embraced all her favourite things – loads of chocolate (a given!), smooth and crunchy praline, Italian meringue frosting, and enough coffee to keep her dancing all night long! It's a labour of love, but what decent cake ever isn't?

Serves 32

For the chocolate layer
60g good-quality cocoa powder
7 large organic eggs
90ml vegetable oil
230g self-raising flour
350g golden caster sugar
1 level tablespoon baking powder

For the malty mocha layer
60g Horlicks
2 tablespoons coffee extract
7 large organic eggs
90ml vegetable oil
230g self-raising flour
350g golden caster sugar
1 level tablespoon baking powder

For the super-light frosting
400g caster sugar
6 large organic egg whites
500g unsalted butter, at room
   temperature, cut into cubes
2 tablespoons coffee extract
1 tablespoon vanilla extract

For the praline, two ways
250g blanched hazelnuts
100g caster sugar

For the ganache drizzle
300g quality dark chocolate (70%
   cocoa solids)
75g unsalted butter
1 tablespoon runny honey
100ml double cream

sea salt

Preheat the oven to 160°C (conventional oven 180°C/Gas Mark 4).

To make this epic cake, you need to make two separate sponge batters. I find it easiest to do these one at a time. For the chocolate layers, mix the cocoa with 175ml of boiling water until nice and smooth, then leave to cool. Separate the eggs, putting the whites into a very clean mixing bowl and the yolks into a large mixing bowl. Whisking the yolks as you go, gradually add the oil until smooth. At this point, gradually whisk in the cooled cocoa mixture. Combine the flour, sugar, baking powder and a good pinch of sea salt, then sift over the yolks, beating until smooth.

Now whisk the egg whites until you get stiff peaks. With a large metal spoon, fold the egg whites into the mix in the other bowl, being careful not to knock the air out as this is what makes your cake beautifully light. Divide the mixture between two 23cm non-stick round, loose-bottomed cake tins. Carefully place in the oven on the middle shelf and bake for about 45 minutes until risen and slightly golden, and a skewer inserted into the centre of the cake comes out clean.

Once done, remove the cakes from the oven (leave the oven on) and cool for a few minutes in the tins, then turn out on to a wire rack. Allow to cool completely while you make the malty mocha sponge batter. To do this, dissolve the Horlicks in 100ml of boiling water along with the coffee extract, mixing until nice and smooth, then leave to cool. Repeat the same process as above, adding the Horlicks mix instead of the cocoa, and bake the second batch of cakes in the same way.

Meanwhile, for the super-light frosting, have a bowl of cold water ready in the sink. Put 300g of caster sugar and 100ml of water into a small saucepan and bring to the boil – don't stir, just give the pan the occasional turn and tilt to help dissolve the sugar. Pop in a sugar thermometer and allow the syrup to boil vigorously – experts say to aim for 121°C, but if you go a little bit over, it won't be the end of the world. As soon as you hit the right temperature, remove the pan from the heat and briefly submerge the bottom half of the pan in the bowl of cold water to stop the temperature rising further.

While the syrup is boiling, start whisking your egg whites in a free-standing electric mixer. When they will stand in stiff peaks, keep the mixer running and add the remaining 100g of sugar. Gradually drizzle in the sugar syrup and continue whisking until the steaming stops. Next, slowly add the butter cubes while whisking. Add the coffee and vanilla extracts, mixing until you have a super-light, glossy frosting. If it looks like it has split at any point, don't worry: it'll come good in the end.

When the second batch of cakes is out of the oven and cooling, scatter the hazelnuts over a baking tray and toast in the oven for 20–25 minutes until dark golden. Meanwhile, place a non-stick pan on a medium heat.

>

Sprinkle a pinch of sugar on to the base: when it has melted, you'll know the pan's ready to go. Gradually add all the sugar, whisking regularly until it has melted and you've got a nice, dark caramel. Tip in the toasted nuts, scatter over a good pinch of sea salt and stir to coat. Pour the nutty caramel out on to greaseproof paper and leave to cool and harden. Blitz half of this praline in a food processor until smooth, and bash the remaining half in a pestle and mortar until fine and crunchy.

To assemble your cake, place a small blob of the smooth praline in the centre of your cake stand or plate – this will keep your cake in place – then pop one of the malty mocha sponge layers on top. Spread a good layer of the smooth praline over the cake and top with a layer of frosting, then scatter a generous layer of crunchy praline evenly over this. Repeat twice more, alternating the sponge layers. Cover the whole outside of the assembled cake with the remaining frosting.

Lastly, make the ganache. Smash up the chocolate and melt with the butter, honey, cream and a pinch of sea salt in a large heatproof bowl set over a pan of gently simmering water until smooth and glossy. Leave the ganache to cool slightly, then pour it over the top of the cake, brushing it to the sides in a circular motion to help it drip down over the edges – any leftover ganache can be drizzled over individual slices, if you like. I've gone for edible flowers and berries, but decorate with whatever you fancy.

• • •

Ashley
Palmer-Watts

'At home I cook from my handwritten book of recipes, collated over 23 years.'

Palmer-Watts

For over a decade Ashley Palmer-Watts played right-hand man to the UK's most celebrated and revered chef Heston Blumenthal. But in 2011 he stepped out of the shadow of the molecular wizard and into the limelight, when Blumenthal put him at the helm of his new London restaurant, Dinner by Heston Blumenthal.

He repaid the faith of his mentor rapidly, instantly gaining rave reviews and collecting two-Michelin-stars within three years for his and Blumenthal's modern interpretation of historic British cuisine. The two researched and created the dishes, but the cooking is all under Palmer-Watts' watch.

Like many chefs, Dorset-born Palmer-Watts' first experience of the restaurant world came as a part-time after-school washer-upper. Having decided on a culinary career, he left school, got himself a job at a well-regarded Dorchester restaurant, learned the fundamentals of cooking and, after eating at and being blown away by Blumenthal's legendary Fat Duck restaurant in Bray, decided that nothing but a job there would do.

So determined was he to work with Blumenthal that he took a job at a local watercress farm while he waited for a position to come up at the Fat Duck. His patience paid off when Palmer-Watts finally joined Blumenthal's brigade in 1999. He thrived on absorbing the Fat Duck's culinary agenda, gaining skills that were to make him the restaurant's head chef by 2001, aged just 25.

From then on, he worked alongside Blumenthal in all the latter's myriad culinary projects, helping to develop and create witty original dishes, sharing Blumenthal's increasing interest in British culinary history, which eventually gave birth to Dinner. Dishes include the unique 'meat fruit' that dates back to Tudor times: essentially chicken liver and foie grois encased in a mandarin jelly so the dish actually looks like a mandarin orange.

At home Palmer-Watts' tastes are far simpler. A roast chicken for his wife and two children suffices at weekends, named 'daddy day' by his son Max. And after a week of gastronomic history, his guilty pleasures run to more modern tastes: crisps and Cheddar cheese, together, go down well for instance, as does one of his mother's specialities: a retro dessert of butterscotch Angel Delight 'with a crumbled flake on top'.

• • •

Secret Food Haunt

Laverstoke Park Farm at Overton in Hampshire is ex-Formula 1 champion Jody Scheckter's 'amazing' organic/biodynamic farm. There's a farm shop on site and a butcher's shop in Twickenham, Middlesex. Beef, lamb, poultry, mozzarella from the farm's own buffalo herd, wild boar, plus organic ale and fruit and vegetables are all sold.

Roast Scallop, Samphire, Pickled Dulse and Clam Broth

You can use palourde or surf clams – whatever is available as long as they aren't too small. Or try this with cockles. The quantities for the pickled dulse will make more than you need for the recipe. Store the remainder in the fridge (it will keep for a couple of weeks) – you can chop it and fry with vegetables such as Tenderstem broccoli, plus garlic and chilli, in olive oil. You'll have leftover vegetable stock too, which can be frozen for other uses. The stock really makes the difference in the recipe so is well worth the time.

Serves 2

olive oil
6 scallops
250g fresh clams, well washed
5g chopped garlic
80ml vegetable stock (see below)
20g samphire
10g rock samphire
5g chopped coriander
20g pickled dulse (see below), chopped, plus a couple of pieces to garnish
30g spring onions (white bulbs with 2cm stalk), finely sliced and soaked in cold water
a squeeze of lemon juice

For the pickled dulse
70ml Chardonnay vinegar
35ml white soy sauce
5g sugar
4g salt
20g dried dulse

For the vegetable stock
20ml olive oil
125g sliced leek (white part only)
100g grated carrots
85g sliced onion
85g grated button mushrooms
40g grated bulb fennel
40g sliced celery
1 small bay leaf
2 sprigs of thyme
10g flat-leaf parsley

First prepare the pickled dulse. Heat the vinegar, white soy sauce and 360ml water in a saucepan. Add the sugar and salt and stir until dissolved. Remove from the heat, pour into a bowl and leave to cool completely.

Meanwhile, thoroughly wash the dried dulse in cold running water to remove any sand. Leave to soak and rehydrate in cold water for 10 minutes. Drain. Add the dulse to the cooled pickling liquid. Leave to pickle in the fridge for 24 hours before using.

Next make the stock. Heat the oil in a large pan and add all the vegetables. Sweat, without colouring, for 5 minutes. Add the bay and thyme along with 750ml cold water. Bring to the boil, skimming off any scum or impurities that rise to the surface, then simmer gently for 25 minutes.

Remove from the heat, add the parsley and set aside to infuse for 20 minutes. Pass the stock through a fine sieve into a bowl. Skim off any fat from the surface of the stock, then keep in the fridge until required.

Heat a litle olive oil in a large, heavy frying pan. Put the scallops in the pan, larger flat side down, and cook over medium–high heat until light golden. Turn the scallops over and cook the other side until light golden. Remove and set aside in a warm place to finish cooking; or, if the scallops are large, put them into a 150°C oven (conventional oven 170°C/Gas Mark 3) to finish cooking for 2–3 minutes. The scallops are done at 50°C internal temperature – check with an instant-read thermometer.

Meanwhile, heat a little more olive oil in the frying pan, then add the clams and cook on a high heat for 1 minute. Add the garlic and cook for another minute. Add the vegetable stock and both types of samphire. Cover the pan and cook for a further minute to open the clams.

Add the chopped coriander, chopped dulse with 1 tablespoon of the pickle liquid, the drained spring onions and a squeeze of lemon juice. Gently mix together, then remove from the heat.

To serve, spoon the clam broth into wide, shallow bowls. Arrange three scallops in each bowl and spoon the clams and samphire over and around. Garnish with a couple of larger pieces of pickled dulse.

• • •

Lamb Chops Grilled Over Charcoal with Cucumber, Broad Beans and Mint

This recipe is spring on a plate. British produce is incredible in the springtime, and the ingredients in this dish really make the most of what's in season. Here both the lamb and cucumber are charcoal-grilled – I use the barbecue at home as much as I do my frying pans. Not many people would think of cooking cucumber, but it's not a new idea. When we go through old recipe books for inspiration at the restaurant, it always crops up. The flavour of hot cucumber – particularly barbecued – is delicious and the texture is firm but moist.

Serves 4

1 garlic clove, halved
8 spring lamb chops or cutlets
olive oil

For the sauce
1 litre fresh lamb stock
1 tablespoon rendered lamb fat
1 sprig of rosemary
1 sprig of mint

To garnish
1 large cucumber
olive oil
3 tablespoons finely chopped shallots
2½ tablespoons Chardonnay vinegar
250g podded broad beans, blanched
    for 10 seconds and peeled
2 tablespoons chopped dill
2 tablespoons chopped flat-leaf parsley

sea salt and coarsely ground black
    pepper

To make the sauce, put the lamb stock into a saucepan and boil to reduce to 100ml. Remove from the heat and whisk in the lamb fat and rosemary sprig. Set aside.

My preferred method of cooking the lamb chops is over charcoal on a barbecue, but you can also roast them in a heavy frying pan over a high heat. If you are going to use a barbecue, prepare the charcoal fire.

Meanwhile, prepare the cucumber for the garnish. Cut off a third of the cucumber and put it through a juicer; you should have about 6 tablespoons juice. Set aside.

Peel the remaining cucumber, then cut across in half. Cut off the four curved 'sides' from each piece of cucumber to leave you with a rectangular 'heart'. Slice the cucumber half-moon 'sides' into 5mm pieces and set aside.

Rub the garlic over the meat of the chops, on both sides, then season with salt and pepper and lightly press the seasoning on to the meat so it sticks. Drizzle over a little olive oil. Grill the lamb chops on the barbecue (or in the hot frying pan) for 2–3 minutes on each side (timing is for medium rare). Wrap the chops in foil and set aside to rest while cooking the garnish.

Season the cucumber hearts and drizzle with olive oil, then place on the barbecue (or in the pan) and cook for 2 minutes per side until lightly coloured and soft. Remove and keep warm.

Pour a thin layer of olive oil into a hot frying pan and add the cucumber pieces. Leave to colour, then gently turn to colour the other sides. Reduce the heat, add the shallots and cook for 2 minutes. Deglaze the pan with the vinegar and reduce until it is almost all gone.

Add 4 tablespoons of the cucumber juice along with the peeled broad beans. Heat gently to ensure the mixture remains moist. Season with salt and pepper and stir in the chopped herbs. Keep warm.

Reheat the sauce, then add the remaining 2 tablespoons of cucumber juice and the sprig of mint.

To serve, cut the cucumber hearts diagonally in half and place a piece in the centre of each large plate. Spoon the broad bean and cucumber mix around and set two chops on top. Remove the mint and rosemary from the sauce, then spoon the sauce over the chops.

• • •

Goat's Cheese Mousse Cake, Spiced Roast Pear and Sorrel

The inspiration behind this recipe was discovering that the medieval Plantagenet court in England had tucked into cheesecake flavoured with 'blomes of elren' or elderflower. It's unbaked to preserve the fresh elderflower flavour, and subtle goat's cheese adds to the savoury character of the dessert.

Serves 8–10

For the base
150g plain Hobnob biscuits
35g dark muscovado sugar
70g unsalted butter, melted
a pinch of salt

For the goat's cheese cream
100g mild goat's cheese without rind
100ml whipping cream, lightly beaten

For the goat's cheese mousse
2 platinum gelatine leaves
100g cream cheese
250ml double goat's cream
20g icing sugar, sifted
60ml elderflower cordial
125ml whipping cream
100g caster sugar
60g egg yolks (from 3–4 medium eggs)

To serve
3 large ripe pears (William's or
   Conference)
40g unsalted butter
½ vanilla pod, split open lengthways
3 star anise
small sprigs of wood or bronze sorrel
   (optional)

To make the base, first lightly oil a 20cm springform tin and line it with greaseproof paper. Blitz the biscuits to crumbs in a food processor, or by putting them in a plastic bag and rolling over them with a rolling pin. In a bowl combine the biscuit crumbs with the sugar, melted butter and salt, mixing well. Press the mixture over the base of the lined tin and place in the fridge to firm up.

Next make the goat's cheese cream. Crumble the cheese into a bowl and add a third of the cream. With a spatula, slowly mix the cheese into the cream. Then gradually add the remaining cream, mixing until smooth. Spread the cheese cream evenly over the biscuit base using a stepped palette knife, leaving a 1cm gap all around the edge so there is no cheese cream on top of the biscuit base there. Return to the fridge to set.

Meanwhile, make the goat's cheese mousse. Soak the gelatine in cold water. Put the cream cheese, goat's cream and icing sugar in a heatproof bowl and set over a pan of barely simmering water. Heat, stirring with a spatula, until melted and thoroughly mixed. Remove from the heat.

Squeeze excess water from the gelatine, then add to the warm cream cheese mix and stir until melted. Stir in the elderflower cordial. Leave to cool down while you carry on with the mousse.

Whip the whipping cream to soft peaks, then keep in the fridge until required.

Put the sugar and 50ml water in a medium saucepan and bring to the boil, stirring to dissolve the sugar. Leave to boil over a moderate heat until the syrup reaches 120°C. While the syrup is boiling, beat the egg yolks in a free-standing electric mixer until thick and creamy in texture.

Take extra care with this next step! When the sugar syrup reaches 120°C, remove the pan from the heat and, with the mixer running, slowly pour the syrup on to the yolks. Continue beating at full speed for 3–5 minutes until the mixture is thickened in texture.

Fold a third of this egg mix into the cooled cream cheese mix and incorporate well before folding in the remaining egg mix. When smooth, carefully fold in the whipped cream, being careful to keep as much air in the mixture as possible. Pour the mousse into the tin to make an even layer on top of the goat's cheese cream. Leave to set in the fridge for at least 3 hours or overnight.

Cut each pear lengthways into quarters, then each piece in half again, yielding eight equal lengths per pear. Use a sharp knife to remove the core from the slices.

Heat a large sauté pan and melt the butter, then carefully lay the pear slices in the pan in a fan-like pattern. Place the vanilla and star anise in amongst the slices. Cook over a medium–high heat until the slices are a light golden colour on both sides, turning them over carefully. Take care not to burn the butter but keep it foaming in order to roast the pears nicely. Remove them from the pan and drain on kitchen paper, then allow to cool a little before serving.

Release the side of the springform tin and remove it. Cut the cheesecake into wedges. To serve, place a piece of cheesecake in the centre of each plate and arrange three slices of roast pear alongside. Finish with a sprinkling of sorrel.

• • •

Neil

Perry

'Great ingredients, simply prepared...'

Perry

Sydney-born Neil Perry's passion for perfection and commitment to showcasing the best seasonal produce his country has to offer has made him one of the most influential chef-restaurateurs in Australia. The founder of Sydney's famous fine-dining restaurant, Rockpool, his empire has expanded over 25 years to include steakhouses, seafood grills, modern Chinese eateries and a restaurant dedicated to Italian regional cuisine in the cities of Sydney, Melbourne and Perth.

But his face and trademark ponytail are recognisable beyond his native shores, thanks to several Australian television shows of his own (some of which have been aired in other countries), appearances on many high-profile international culinary programmes and his creation of first class and business menus for Australia's national airline, Qantas.

It was Perry's father, a butcher, who first instilled a devotion to quality produce in his young son. However, he trained first as a hairdresser before a job as a waiter introduced him to the hospitality world and kick-started his career, initially as a successful restaurant manager at Sydney restaurant Sails in the suburb of McMahon's Point. It wasn't long, though, before a love of food drew him into the kitchen and after learning his trade for several years under some of Australia's most respected chefs, he opened Rockpool in 1989 with cousin and business partner Trish Richards.

In just six months it won Best New Restaurant in the influential the *Sydney Morning Herald*'s Good Food Guide; and went on to garner many more national and international accolades over the years.

Secret Food Haunt
Room 10 Espresso café in Sydney's inner-suburb of Pott's Point. Being a 'hole in the wall' with a miniscule kitchen its food is limited mostly to 'superb' open and closed sandwiches, all made with top-notch produce. Breakfasts (and coffee) are a specialty: soy and linseed toast with mashed avocado and boiled eggs is typical. A delivery service is operated as well.

Perry is still based in Sydney, where he lives with his wife Samantha and their three beautiful daughters. Weekend relaxing takes the form of brunching at their favourite café or a Sunday night meal at their local Korean restaurant, often enjoying an abalone steamboat. If the family eats at home then 'simple things' – roast chicken, noodles, a stir-fry or taco – made with 'great ingredients' win out. A peek in the freezer might also see some frozen Kit Kats – Perry's guilty sweet treat – squirrelled away.

Despite family commitments, the demands of his seven restaurants and other business interests, Perry always finds time to support several, mainly children's, charities, and in 2013 was made a Member of the Order of Australia (one of Australia's highest public honours) in recognition of both his culinary achievements and his work in the community.

Lobster and Bulghur Wheat Salad
with Harissa Mayonnaise

This is a tribute to all those wonderful North African flavours and textures - preserved lemons, punchy harissa, bulghur wheat, coriander – and to the delicate sweetness of lobster. You can buy harissa (or the preserved lemons that go into it), but take the time to make your own and you will be rewarded, this dish is equally delicious with cooked prawns, or even poached or roast chicken...

Serves 4 as a light lunch

1 whole fresh lobster, about 650g
salt

For the preserved lemons
5 fresh, ripe unwaxed lemons
80g sea salt

For the harissa
3g each coriander seeds and fennel
  seeds
5g cumin seeds
15g fresh garlic cloves, finely sliced
300g red peppers, cut into 3cm squares
25ml olive oil
10g light palm sugar, finely chopped
10ml fish sauce
2g chilli powder

For the bulghur wheat salad
70g fine bulghur wheat
2 small, ripe vine tomatos, seeded and
  cut into 1cm dice
150g baby spinach leaves, thinly sliced
1 small red pepper, roasted, peeled and
  coarsely chopped
handful coriander leaves, chopped
25g finely sliced preserved lemon peel
  (see above)

For the lemon dressing
25ml freshly squeezed lemon juice
80ml extra virgin olive oil
1g finely grated lemon zest
2g Dijon mustard
1g caster sugar
sea salt and freshly ground black pepper

For the harissa mayonnaise
15g harissa (see above)
75g good-quality mayonnaise

First prepare the preserved lemons. Cut the lemons in half and juice them, then cut into quarters. Put the juice and quartered lemons in a pan with the salt and enough water to cover. Bring to the boil and simmer for about 5 minutes. Leave the lemons to cool in the brine. Pack the lemons into a sterilised jar, cover with brine and keep in the fridge (the preserved lemons will last for months and can be used in numerous recipes). To use the lemons, remove and discard the flesh and white pith, then chop or slice the peel.

Next make the harissa for the mayonnaise. Carefully roast the spice seeds in a small pan until fragrant, then grind finely in a spice mill; set aside. Sweat the garlic and red peppers in the olive oil in an uncovered pan over very low heat for about 30 minutes until very soft, stirring often to prevent sticking. Increase the heat, add the palm sugar and cook, stirring, for about 5 minutes until well caramelised – the mixture should go a reddish brown. Add the fish sauce, roasted spices and chilli powder and stir for 2 minutes. Allow to cool slightly before blitzing in a food processor until smooth. When cold, keep in a sterilised jar in the fridge (the harissa can be stored for several weeks).

Next prepare the lobster. Put it in the freezer or immerse in a bowl of iced water for 20 minutes, to send it to sleep. Fill a large saucepan with salted water and bring to the boil. Put the lobster into the water and bring back to the boil, then remove from the heat. Set aside for about 6 minutes. Remove the lobster and plunge into a bowl of iced salted water. When cold, remove the meat from the claws and tail. Clean the entrails from the tail meat and slice into 1cm medallions. Set the lobster meat aside in the fridge.

To make the salad, put the bulghur in a mixing bowl, pour over 125ml boiling water and stir, then leave to soak for 30 minutes. Drain off any unabsorbed water and squeeze the bulghur dry in a clean tea towel. Return to the dried bowl, add the remaining salad ingredients and toss gently to combine.

While the bulghur is soaking, make the lemon dressing and harissa mayonnaise. Combine all the dressing ingredients in a bowl with 1g each sea salt and freshly ground black pepper and whisk until well combined. In another bowl mix together the mayonnaise ingredients.

To serve, toss the bulghur wheat salad with half of the lemon dressing, then add more dressing if needed. Spoon the salad on to serving plates and top with the lobster medallions and claw meat. Finish each serving with a spoonful of harissa mayonnaise.

• • •

Slow-roasted Sirloin with Anchovy Butter, Potato Gratin and Baby Carrots

I've eaten this dish all my life in bistros and American steakhouses, then I started making it at home. It's the best way to cook beef - slowly so you have more control. You get the crust and the melting interior. I find anchovy butter is great with all meats and barbecued meats especially. You can also do this recipe with pork. If you can't get bintje potatoes, substitute them with another waxy variety, like kipfler.

Serves 4

1 beef sirloin joint, weighing about 800g, fat removed, boned and rolled
olive oil
sea salt and freshly ground black pepper

For the anchovy butter
20g garlic cloves, finely chopped
1 tablespoon olive oil
2g sea salt
60g unsalted butter, diced
2ml (about ½ teaspoon) fresh lemon juice
2g roughly chopped flat-leaf parsley leaves
30g (drained weight) good-quality anchovy fillets in oil, drained and chopped

For the potato gratin
a small knob of unsalted butter
1 garlic clove, finely chopped
160ml double cream
a pinch of chopped thyme leaves
500g Bintje potatoes, peeled and cut into 1mm slices
15g unsalted butter, melted

For the carrots
20 baby carrots, trimmed and scrubbed
2 tablespoons extra virgin olive oil

First make the anchovy butter. Put the garlic cloves in a small saucepan with the olive oil and salt. Heat very gently until the garlic has softened but not coloured. Remove from the heat, drain off the olive oil and cool.

Put the butter in a food processor and blitz until softened. Add the softened garlic and the lemon juice and mix into the butter. Add the parsley and anchovies and gently mix through. Transfer the anchovy butter to a bowl and set aside at room temperature.

Next make the potato gratin. Preheat the oven to 180°C (conventional oven 200°C/Gas Mark 6). Melt the knob of butter in a thick-based saucepan, add the garlic with a pinch of salt and cook gently for about 4 minutes until softened. Add a quarter of the cream and the thyme leaves and heat through. Pour this garlic cream into a large bowl and stir in the remaining cream. Add the sliced potatoes and mix gently but thoroughly to cover all of the slices with cream.

Brush the base and sides of a small shallow baking dish with some of the melted butter. Arrange the potato slices, overlapping, in lines down the dish (reserve the cream), drizzling melted butter between the layers. Pour the reserved cream over the top. Bake the gratin for 50 minutes to 1 hour, until lightly browned and the potatoes are tender. When ready, remove the gratin from the oven and cut into four portions, then keep hot.

While the gratin is baking, season the sirloin all over with sea salt. Heat a little oil in a heavy frying pan and quickly sear the joint until browned on all sides. Transfer to a roasting tin. In a bowl, toss the carrots with the oil and 1 teaspoon of salt, then spread out in the roasting tin with the sirloin.

Place in the oven alongside the gratin and roast for 30–35 minutes until the internal temperature of the meat reaches 57°C (check with an instant-read thermometer). Remove from the oven and season with freshly ground black pepper. Cover the sirloin with foil and leave to rest for about 20 minutes in a warm place. Keep the carrots hot.

Cut the sirloin into four equal slices. Place a generous spoonful of anchovy butter on top of each slice of sirloin and serve with the baby carrots and potato gratin.

• • •

Chocolate and Caramel Tart

This tart is delicious with creme anglaise, or with a rich vanilla ice-cream. If you prefer individual tarts, use mini tart shells instead of one large one. The tart will need to cool in the fridge for three hours.

Makes 1 tart to serve 10

For the sweet pastry
225g plain flour
80g icing sugar
25g ground almonds
1g sea salt
125g unsalted butter, at room temperature, cut into small pieces
20g egg yolk (from about 1 large egg)
20ml milk
2g vanilla extract

For the caramel filling
220g caster sugar
80ml double cream, warmed
80g unsalted butter, coarsely chopped
1g sea salt

For the chocolate mousse
310ml whipping cream
225g dark chocolate (70% cocoa solids), chopped
105g caster sugar
40g egg yolks (from about 2 large eggs)
60g whole egg (about 1 large egg)

For the chocolate topping
50ml milk
100g dark chocolate (70% cocoa solids), chopped
20g unsalted butter, softened
15g liquid glucose

First make the pastry case. Sift the flour and icing sugar into a mixing bowl and add the ground almonds, salt and butter. Mix until the butter is incorporated, using your fingers if you wish. Add the egg yolk, milk and vanilla and gently mix until the pastry begins to come together. Remove from the bowl and briefly mix to form a smooth dough. Wrap in clingfilm and chill for at least 30 minutes.

Use soft butter to grease a 24cm loose-based tart tin. Roll out the pastry on a lightly floured worktop to 3–4mm thick and use to line the tin, pushing the pastry into the corners and ensuring that the sides are even and come up to just above the rim of the tin. Chill for at least 30 minutes.

Preheat the oven to 160°C (conventional oven 180°C/Gas Mark 4). Line the inside of the pastry case with silicone paper or baking parchment and fill with rice or baking beans. Blind bake the tart case for about 18 minutes until set and golden brown at the edges, then remove the paper and beans and bake for a further 5–10 minutes to colour the base. Set aside to cool.

Next make the caramel filling. Combine the sugar and 150ml water in a heavy-based saucepan and stir over low heat until the sugar dissolves. Increase the heat to high and bubble, brushing down the sides of the pan with a wet pastry brush, until the mixture caramelises to a deep golden colour. Remove from the heat and add the cream, butter and sea salt (be careful as the mixture will spit). Stir to mix. Immediately pour into a stainless steel bowl to prevent further cooking. Leave to cool.

Pour the caramel filling into the tart case (still in its tin). Cover and refrigerate for about 2 hours until firm.

Meanwhile, make the chocolate mousse. Place 200ml of the cream in a mixing bowl and whip until the cream is firm and will hold a peak. Set aside in the fridge. Put the chocolate and remaining cream in a large heatproof bowl and set over a pan of simmering water. Heat gently until the chocolate has melted, then stir until smoothly blended. The chocolate should be just warm but not too hot. Remove from the heat.

Put the sugar in a thick-based pan and barely cover with warm water. Heat until the sugar dissolves, then bring to the boil, brushing down the sides of the pan to prevent crystallisation. When the sugar mix has begun to boil, put the egg yolks and whole egg into a mixing bowl and begin to whisk on a high speed (it's easiest to do this in a free-standing electric mixer).

Check the temperature of the boiling sugar syrup with a thermometer. When it reaches 121°C, remove the pan from the heat. At this stage, the eggs should be pale, aerated and foamy. Reduce the speed of the mixer and slowly pour the hot sugar syrup into the bowl, over the eggs being whisked – avoid the syrup touching the side of the bowl and the moving whisk. When all the syrup has been added, increase the speed to just above medium and whisk until the mixture cools down.

Transfer the egg mixture to the bowl of melted chocolate and gently fold through, taking care not to knock out any air. Gently fold in the whipped cream.

Pour or pipe the mousse on to the set caramel filling in the tart case and spread out evenly; the surface should be smooth and come to just below the top of the tart edges. Return to the fridge to chill for 2 hours until firm.

For the chocolate topping, heat the milk (do not boil). Put the chocolate and butter in a bowl, pour the hot milk over and stir until smooth and well mixed. Add the glucose and mix through. Set aside to cool until just barely warm.

To finish the tart, spoon the warm chocolate topping over the mousse and tilt the tart so the topping flows to cover the whole of the mousse evenly. Chill until set.

• • •

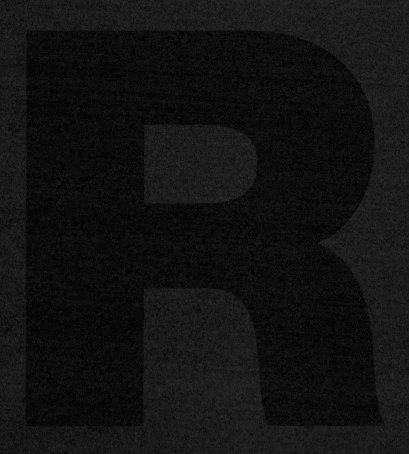

Gordon
Ramsay

'I have a huge collection of cookbooks and love them all.'

Ramsay

Few chefs have the international profile of Gordon Ramsay. A superlative chef, he won the much-sought-after award of three-Michelin-stars at the tender age of 31 at his flagship London eaterie, Restaurant Gordon Ramsay, the youngest chef to do so in the UK at that time. He then proceeded to build an international restaurant empire and a television career as host on a number of reality and culinary shows on both sides of the Atlantic.

His restaurant realm of over 20 businesses stretches far beyond London – to New York, Las Vegas, Paris, the Middle East and the Far East – and includes gastropubs, steak houses and, more recently, his Bread Street Kitchen all-day dining restaurants.

Ramsay is famous for his straight talking. He's been reported as having robust views about vegetarians on more than one occasion, but in truth he's adamant about being 'absolutely OK with vegetarians! Really!' More than that, he believes that vegetables are underrated – 'grilled with a bit of spice they are a great part of a meal'.

As a young teenager he had ambitions to be a professional footballer in the UK; however, injury soon made Ramsay consider another path. After being mentored by some of the great trail-blazers of London cuisine – including Albert Roux and Marco Pierre White – in the late 1990s he struck out on his own, perfecting his brand of elegant modern Franco-Italian cooking along the way, picking up countless culinary awards as he did so.

Away from the kitchen, Ramsay is famous for his marathon running and these days he adds 'long bike rides' to his relaxation routine – all part of getting ready for Iron Man triathlons. A glass or two of cold pressed juice at breakfast sets him up for his exertions. Being so obsessed by exercise, however, doesn't stop him admitting to having a 'weakness' for cars: or a guilty yearning for burgers!

Home life is centred around his wife, Tana, and their four children. His tip for home cooks is to try beef Wellington if you're after a wow factor on the dinner table: 'It's really impressive and gets the family together.'

• • •

Secret Food Haunt
The Farmers' Market, The Grove, Los Angeles. An outdoor market, established originally in 1934 and located in the Fairfax district of the city, it has local farm produce of every kind alongside restaurants, cafés and food stalls. Latin American and Asian food cuisine is particularly good here.

Slow-roast Pork with Apple and Lavender Sauce

Slow cooking renders pork shoulder meltingly tender and the sauce balances the richness perfectly. If you don't have any lavender, replace the caster sugar with lavender sugar, which you can buy from selected supermarkets and delis.

Serves 6–8

1 x 2kg boned shoulder of pork
3 medium onions, halved
4–5 bay leaves
olive oil for the tin
200ml dry cider

For the apple and lavender sauce
4 cooking apples
30g butter
30g caster sugar
flowers stripped from a few lavender stems
sea salt and freshly ground black pepper

Preheat the oven to its highest setting. Pat the pork rind dry with kitchen paper, then score at 5mm intervals. Rub all over with salt and pepper, massaging the seasoning into the cuts. Scatter the onion halves and bay leaves in a lightly oiled roasting tin and lay the pork on top, skin side up.

Roast for 20–25 minutes until the skin starts to blister and crisp, then lower the oven setting to 130°C (conventional oven 150°C/Gas Mark 2). If there is any rendered fat, remove from the tin, then pour the cider around the pork. Cover with foil and roast for a further 4–5 hours until the pork is very tender. Several times during roasting, lift the foil and baste the sides of the joint with the pan juices. The pork is done when it can easily be shredded with a fork.

While the pork is roasting, make the sauce. Peel, core and roughly chop the apples. Melt the butter in a saucepan and add the apples with the sugar and lavender flowers. Cook over a medium–high heat for 10–15 minutes until soft and pulpy, stirring occasionally and adding a little water if needed. Sieve if you prefer a very smooth sauce. Season with salt and freshly ground pepper, and set aside, ready to reheat gently before serving.

When the pork is cooked, take it out of the oven. Slice off the rind and place it on a baking sheet. Turn the oven to its highest setting and roast the rind for 10–15 minutes until it turns to a crisp, golden crackling. Meanwhile, cover the pork shoulder loosely with foil and leave to rest in a warm place for 15–20 minutes.

Slice the pork shoulder thickly and serve with the pan juices, warm apple and lavender sauce and broken shards of crisp crackling.

• • •

Lamb Stew with Shallots, Smoked Bacon and Prunes

This recipe is ideal to share with family and friends. It is incredibly simple to make with minimal fuss, but still packs great flavour. The smoky bacon cuts through the rich lamb with the spices adding a little warmth and the prunes giving that edge of sweetness.

Serves 4

1 boned leg of lamb, about 650g
2–3 tablespoon olive oil
250g smoked streaky bacon, chopped
400g shallots or red onions, sliced
1½ teaspoons caster sugar
a generous splash of dry white wine
1 cinnamon stick
1 teaspoon ground ginger
150g soft pitted prunes, halved
500ml lamb stock
chopped parsley, to garnish
sea salt and freshly ground black
    pepper

Trim any fat and sinew from the leg of lamb, then cut the meat into bite-sized pieces. Season with salt and pepper. Heat some of the oil in a large, heavy-based frying pan. When it is very hot sear the pieces of lamb until browned on all sides (fry in batches to avoid over-crowding the pan). As each batch is browned, remove from the pan and set aside.

Add a little more oil to the pan and fry the chopped bacon for 3–4 minutes until lightly browned. Tip in the shallots and cook over a medium heat, stirring frequently, for 4–6 minutes until the shallots begin to soften. Add the sugar and a little salt and pepper, then cook for a further 2–3 minutes until the shallots are lightly caramelised.

Deglaze the pan with the wine, scraping the bottom of the pan with a wooden spoon to loosen any sediment. Let the wine boil down until syrupy. Return the lamb to the pan and add the cinnamon, ginger and half the prunes. Stir to mix. Pour in the stock and bring to a simmer. Cover the pan, reduce the heat to low and cook for 1 hour, stirring every now and then.

Add the remaining prunes to the pan and cook for a further 30 minutes until the lamb is very tender. Taste and adjust the seasoning before serving garnished with parsley and serve with mashed potato or couscous.

• • •

Herb-Buttered Chicken
with Citrus Breadcrumbs

This is great with a crunchy light salad of watercress and radish.

Serves 4

1 large chicken, about 2.5kg
1 large onion, halved
½ orange
1 head of garlic (unpeeled), halved
    horizontally
a few bay leaves
a few sprigs of thyme
olive oil for drizzling

For the herb butter
a small bunch of flat-leaf parsley,
    chopped
a small bunch of tarragon, chopped
1 tablespoon thyme leaves
250g butter, softened to room
    temperature

For the citrus breadcrumbs
½ loaf of day-old white bread, about
    300g, crusts removed
grated zest of 1 orange
grated zest of 1 lemon
olive oil for cooking
50g pancetta (about 7–8 rashers),
    chopped
½ onion, finely diced
a few sprigs of thyme
200g pine nuts
150g butter, cut into cubes
a squeeze of lemon juice
sea salt and freshly ground black
    pepper

First make the herb butter by mixing the herbs into the soft butter with plenty of seasoning. Spoon the flavoured butter into a piping bag fitted with a basic piping nozzle.

Working from the neck end, use the fingers of one hand to loosen the skin over the breasts, without tearing the skin. On each side of the breastbone, move your hand towards the lower side of the breast and on to the thighs, to separate the skin from the flesh. You want to create a large pocket for the herb butter on both sides of the breastbone. Pipe the butter into the pockets, over the breasts and thighs. Gently massage the herb butter over the flesh to spread evenly.

Preheat the oven to 200°C (conventional oven 220°C/Gas Mark 7). Season the cavity of the chicken, then stuff with the onion, orange, garlic, bay leaves and thyme sprigs. Tuck the legs under the neck skin to secure them in place, or tie with kitchen string. Place the chicken, breast side up, in a large roasting tray. Drizzle over a little olive oil and season well.

Roast for 10–15 minutes until the skin is crisp and golden, then lower the oven setting to 160°C (conventional oven 180°C/Gas Mark 4) and roast for a further 25 minutes per kg, basting occasionally until cooked. To test if the chicken is cooked, insert a skewer into the thickest part of the thigh: the juices that run out should be clear, not at all pink.

While the chicken is roasting, make the breadcrumbs. Tear up the bread roughly and blitz to coarse crumbs in a food processor. Add the orange and lemon zests and season well. Pulse a few times to mix, then set aside. Heat a little olive oil in a large frying pan and fry the pancetta for 1 minute. Toss in the onion, thyme and pine nuts and cook for 3–4 minutes. Add the butter around the edge of the pan. Allow the butter to melt and foam and then turn a golden brown before adding the breadcrumbs. Mix well and cook, tossing frequently, for 5 minutes until the crumbs are nicely golden. Squeeze over a little lemon juice, discard the thyme stalks and adjust the seasoning. Keep warm.

When the chicken is done, remove it from the oven, cover with foil and leave to rest for at least 15 minutes before carving the breast and cutting up the thighs and legs. Strain the cooking juices through a fine sieve and drizzle over the chicken. Serve with the citrus breadcrumbs.

• • •

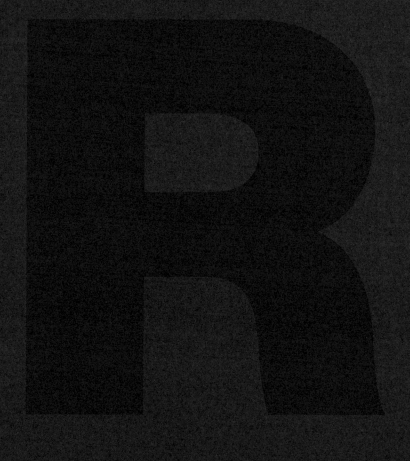

Eric
Ripert

'When it comes to cooking, I'm a minimalist.'

Ripert

aw, barely touched and lightly cooked. This is Eric Ripert's touchstone checklist for the fish and seafood dishes that lie at the heart of the success of Le Bernardin, the legendary New York restaurant that he co-owns and which is often referred to as the city's 'Temple of Seafood'.

Ripert – a Frenchman at the heart of New York's restaurant scene – began his life-long affair with seafood in his Mediterranean hometown of Antibes where he learned the rudiments of cooking from his mother and grandmother. (He still cooks his mother's coq au vin when off-duty at home – 'it's damn good!'). He later imbued the cuisine traditions of the Pyrenees after his family moved across the border to Andorra.

There never was any doubt that he would train as a chef and by the age of 17 he was working in Paris, first at the famous La Tour d'Argent and then at the equally iconic Jamin under one of France's most celebrated chefs, Joël Robuchon. By the early 1990s Ripert had crossed the Atlantic to further his career and it wasn't long before his talent was recognised by the late, great Gilbert Le Coze, owner of Le Bernardin. Success wasn't long in coming, and under his guidance the restaurant became a multi-award-winner, with a five-star rating from *New York* magazine and the bestowing of three-Michelin-stars being just two of the restaurant's decorations.

On weekends off he revels in the chance to enjoy time with his wife and son – long walks are routine – and he's partial to 'a good tequila' in the peace and quiet. Ripert's not averse to popping a few gummy bears, either (half a pound in minutes isn't unusual – 'I don't feel guilt, only pleasure!'). Most of all, he likes to do 'absolutely nothing!' and enjoy the passing seasons – 'who doesn't love sitting by the fire on a snowy day in January?'

• • •

Secret Food Haunt
Agata & Valentina, a store close to where Ripert lives in New York (there are two stores, one on the Upper East Side, the other in Greenwich Village). Great for meat and really fresh seafood.

Tuna Carpaccio

This method of preparing the carpaccio is very interesting as it allows you to use tuna instead of meat. It's very light and refined with a lot of flavour.

Serves 4

350g sushi-quality yellowfin tuna fillet

For the garnish
4 tablespoons extra virgin olive oil
2 teaspoons finely chopped shallots
2 tablespoons thinly sliced chives
1 lemon, cut in half
fine sea salt and freshly ground white
  pepper

Using a very sharp knife, cut the tuna into 5mm-thick slices. Lay a large sheet of clingfilm (at least 60 x 90cm) on the work surface. Arrange the tuna pieces on the clingfilm, leaving 2.5cm space between each slice. Cover the tuna with another large sheet of clingfilm. Gently pound the tuna with a kitchen mallet until there is a very thin and even layer of tuna about 3mm thick.

Cut out a 12.5cm diameter round template from card. Use this and a sharp knife to cut out four discs of tuna, cutting through the fish and both layers of clingfilm. Chill the tuna discs, kept flat on a tray, for at least 30 minutes (the fish can be pounded and cut a few hours ahead of time).

You will need four round plates with an inside diameter of 12.5cm. Chill these.

To serve, place a tuna disc on one hand and peel off the top piece of clingfilm. Invert the tuna on to a plate, then peel off the other piece of clingfilm. Season the tuna with salt and pepper and brush with extra virgin olive oil. Sprinkle shallots and chives on the pounded tuna discs and squeeze lemon juice over each portion.

• • •

Barely Cooked Salmon with Poached White Asparagus, Peas, Broad Beans and Chervil Emulsion

I love the technique of cooking unilaterally. In this recipe, the technique enhances the flavour of the salmon. The chervil sauce is a good way of capturing the essence of the chervil, which has a very delicate flavour.

Serves 4

8 x 90g pieces of salmon fillet, 2.5cm wide

For the sauce
150g chervil leaves
225g unsalted butter, cut into 1cm cubes

For the asparagus
4 spears jumbo white asparagus
1 teaspoon caster sugar
15g unsalted butter

For the peas and broad beans
75g podded fresh peas
75g podded fresh broad beans
a small knob of unsalted butter

fine sea salt and freshly ground white pepper

First make the sauce. Drop the chervil leaves into boiling water and blanch for 10 seconds. Drain and immediately refresh in an ice bath. Remove from the water and drain. Set aside.

Bring 2 tablespoons water to the boil in a saucepan. Lower the heat to a low simmer and whisk in the butter, two cubes at a time, to 'mount' the butter. Once all the butter has been added, transfer to a blender. Add the chervil and blitz for 30 seconds. Season to taste with salt and pepper. Reserve at room temperature.

To prepare the asparagus, peel the stalks, then cut the spears on the diagonal into 1cm-thick slices. Put the asparagus in a medium saucepan and pour in just enough water to cover. Add the sugar and butter, and season with salt and pepper. Bring to the boil, then turn down to just below boiling and cook for 5–10 minutes until the asparagus is just tender. Remove from the liquid and set aside; reserve a little liquid for reheating.

Next prepare the peas and beans. Drop the peas into boiling water and blanch for 2 minutes. Drain and refresh in an ice bath. Split the skin to pop out each pea. For the broad beans, blanch them for 2 minutes, drain and refresh, then slip them out of their skins. Combine the peas and beans in a small saucepan with the butter and 1 teaspoon water. Season and set aside.

Season the salmon fillets on both sides, then place them cut side down in a sauté pan. Add enough salted water to the pan to come a quarter of the way up the sides of the salmon. Turn the heat to medium–high and poach the salmon for 5–6 minutes until the top of the salmon is warm and a metal skewer inserted into the centre of the fish for 5 seconds feels barely warm when touched to your lip. The salmon should be rare. Lift out the fish and drain briefly on kitchen paper.

While the salmon is poaching, reheat the chervil sauce, asparagus, peas and beans.

To plate the dish, place two pieces of salmon in the centre of each plate. Surround each piece of salmon with three pieces of asparagus. Fill the negative space with the peas and beans. Aerate the sauce with a hand blender to make it frothy, then sauce the plates. Serve immediately.

• • •

Squid Basquaise

My father used to live in the Basque country and I'm always inspired by that region. This is an adaption of a classic basquaise and by adding squid, it makes it a little more fancy.

Serves 4

For the squid

12 medium-sized squid, tentacles
  discarded and tubes/bodies cleaned
2 tablespoons extra virgin olive oil
2 sprigs of thyme
2 garlic cloves, halved
1 shallot, sliced into thick pieces
1 teaspoon ground espelette pepper
1 lemon, halved

For the basquaise

3 tablespoons olive oil
80g finely diced onion
1 teaspoon finely chopped garlic
40g finely diced cured ham (Parma
  or Serrano)
60g finely diced red pepper
60g finely diced yellow pepper
205g skinned, seeded and diced
  tomatoes
1 teaspoon chopped thyme leaves

For the sauce

2 tablespoons canola/rapeseed oil
115g sliced onion
8 garlic cloves, sliced
60g Serrano ham, cut in large pieces
120g diced red pepper
120g diced yellow pepper
155g skinned, seeded and diced
  tomatoes

For the fried parsley

500ml canola/rapeseed oil
12 sprigs of parsley

fine sea salt, freshly ground black and
  white pepper, and ground espelette
  pepper

To prepare the squid, cut open each tube/body lengthways and open it out flat. Scrape both sides and clean well. On the side that was the inside of the tube, evenly score the flesh with a very sharp knife to create a cross-hatch pattern, making sure not to cut all the way through.

Put the squid in a bowl with the extra virgin olive oil, thyme, garlic, shallot and espelette pepper. Mix together, then leave to marinate in the fridge for at least 1 hour.

Meanwhile, make the basquaise. Heat the olive oil in a heavy-based saucepan, add the onion and sweat over a low–medium heat until tender. Add the garlic and continue cooking for a minute, then add the ham and peppers. When the peppers are soft, add the tomatoes and thyme. Simmer over a low heat, stirring often, for 30 minutes. Season to taste with salt, white pepper and espelette pepper. Remove from the heat and keep warm.

Make the sauce while the basquaise is simmering. Heat the oil in a medium saucepan and sweat the onion, garlic, ham and peppers over a low–medium heat for 10–15 minutes until the vegetables are tender. Season with salt and espelette pepper. Stir in the tomatoes and cook for 5 minutes. Add just enough water to cover, then cook for another 5 minutes. Blend with a hand blender until smooth. Sieve through a chinois, pushing down with a ladle to press though some of the pulp. Adjust the seasoning and keep warm.

To fry the parsley, heat the oil in a medium saucepan to 180°C. Add the parsley. Be careful because the hot oil will pop and crackle. Deep-fry for 1–2 minutes until the parsley stops bubbling. Remove from the oil and drain on kitchen paper. Season with salt. Keep warm.

Heat a griddle or a ridged cast-iron grill pan until very hot. Lift the squid out of the marinade, removing all the aromatics, and lay out flat on a tray. The squid should still have a coating of oil from the marinade. Season the squid on both sides with salt and white pepper.

From this point on, you will need to work quickly. Cooking one or two at a time, add the pieces of squid, scored side down, to the hot pan. Immediately press the squid flat with a spatula and cook for 5 seconds. Flip the squid on to the other side to cook for 1 second. When you flip the squid, it will curl into the shape of a wheel. Remove from the pan and keep warm. Repeat until all of the squid is cooked. Finish all the squid by squeezing the lemon juice over the top.

To plate, place three quenelles of basquaise on each plate. Put a piece of squid between each quenelle. Garnish with fried parsley, sauce and serve immediately.

• • •

Joan & Jordi
Roca

'When we go out we look for authentic and honest places.'

Roca

Since the late 1990s, Spanish cuisine has spearheaded the fine-dining march into the 21st century. And one of its shining lights is the three-Michelin-star restaurant El Celler de Can Roca in Girona, in the north-east corner of the country. Here, three brothers – Joan, Josep and Jordi Roca – are responsible for creating what is universally held to be an unforgettable and outstanding dining experience, Joan and Jordi in the kitchen and pastry kitchen, Josep via the wine cellar.

So revered is the two chefs' particular and unique talent of fusing molecular know-how with the traditions of their region and the produce of the country surrounding their city, that El Celler de Can Roca was named the greatest restaurant in the world in 2013 by *Restaurant* magazine's influential annual San Pellegrino World's 50 Best Restaurants list. The following year Jordi had the title of the World's Best Pastry Chef bestowed upon him at the same awards.

However, El Celler is really the culmination not just of three brothers but of three generations of the Roca family, as both the boys' parents and grandparents are famous for the family eaterie, Restaurant Can Roca. In fact, when it first opened in 1986 El Celler adjoined its older sibling in the Taila suburb of Girona (it relocated to its present inner city site in Can Sunyer in 2007).

Naturally, Joan and Jordi (the eldest and youngest of the brothers, respectively) took their first steps in the art of cooking at the apron strings of their mother and grandmother before going on to formal training at Girona's catering college. The traditional dishes they learned from these two remarkable women include, in Jordi's case, the classic Crema Catalana and in Joan's case, 'more than a dish', but how to make and use the Catalan paste, picada. 'A "picada" is the ending,' he explains, 'the last aroma added to finish the cooking process. It consists of several ingredients minced in the mortar. The most commonly used ingredients are garlic, parsley, saffron, hazelnuts, pine nuts, biscuits, chocolate, nyora peppers, chicken or monkfish liver, dry or toasted bread crumbs.'

Joan also has fond memories of making butifarra sausages with his mother at Can Roca. Joan and Jordi's own cuisine, though, while it respects and holds in affection their culinary heritage, is of an altogether more challenging and wondrous nature. It runs to caramelised olives presented on a bonsai tree, fish masquerading as pork, edible football pitches, dishes inspired by perfumes and chickens in paper rockets.

They still join their parents for lunch at Can Roca every day, but also try out other 'authentic and honest' local restaurants for inspiration and enjoyment, often in the company of friends or family. Jordi has indulged a lifetime passion for ice cream, too, launching his own Willy Wonker-esque ice cream parlour, Rocambolesc, in Girona, Barcelona and Madrid. Here, apart from fantastic ice creams, Jordi's imagination has created hot ice cream filled buns and ice cream muffins.

With the culinary world at their feet – and a commitment, particularly in Joan's case, to education in their field at home and around the world – the brothers' most precious, but rare, commodity is free time to spend with their wives and, in Joan's case, his two children. When he is able to cook at home Jordi opts for dishes like cebiche tacos, while Joan favours traditional rice dishes, often cooked with the 'subtle harmony' of his son and daughter.

Unsurprisingly, when it comes to must-have store cupboard ingredients and can't-do-without gadgets, pastry maestro Jordi is never without sugar or a blender: Joan, on the other hand, will never run short of olive oil or misplace his knives. He also keeps a copy of Harold McGee's influential *On Food and Cooking: the Science and Lore of the Kitchen* (the bible for all molecular-inspired chefs) on his bookshelf.

Jordi, though, prefers to keep a selection of his elder brother's books to hand, particularly Joan's masterly tome about sous-vide cooking. 'He's my culinary hero.' That aside, he fantasises about cooking for the fictitious Willy Wonka of chocolate factory fame. Naturally!

• • •

Secret Food Haunt

Joan: Le Llotja de Palamos, in Girona is the Mediterranean city-port's local fish auction market. Fish of every kind are landed here but it's particularly famous for shellfish such as prawns, shrimp and squid.

Jordi: El Mercat del Lleo, in Girona's Plaça Calvet i Rubalcaba is a food market selling traditional Catalan produce, everything from fresh fruit and vegetables to olives and seafood. Salted cod in many guises is a speciality. It's open daily and is used by local chefs and residents alike.

Chestnut Purée, Wild Mushrooms and Hints of Aniseed

This dish captures fully the warm flavours and aromas of autumn.
It's something to enjoy in tranquillity by the fireside.

Serves 8

100g unpeeled chestnuts
1 x 200g sweet potato
500g peeled chestnuts
85g unsalted butter

A mixture of mushrooms
30g saffron milk cap
20g horns of plenty/trompettes de la mort
30g chanterelles
30g enoki

200g turnip, roughly chopped
seeds from 1 pomegranate
chervil oil
purple shiso leaves, fennel or tarragon leaves, or micro beetroot leaves (optional)

Roast the unpeeled chestnuts until tender, ideally in the ashes of an open fire. Peel and slice them. Set aside for the garnish.

Preheat the oven to 160°C (conventional oven 180°C/Gas Mark 4). Bake the sweet potato, in its skin, until it's completely soft. Peel the sweet potato, then blend it until smooth (add a bit of water to help make it smooth, if necessary).

Boil the peeled chestnuts in a pan of salted water for 10 minutes. Drain and purée them in a blender keeping it rather stiff, then pass through a sieve. While the chestnut purée is still warm, emulsify 300g of it with 60g of the butter – add the butter and whisk to incorporate. Let it cool down so it has solidified a little. Pass this mixture through a flour sieve: it will come out in thin threads on the base of the sieve. Gently remove the threads with a spatula and place on the serving plates to form a carpet-like display. Set aside.

To prepare the mushrooms, halve the saffron milk cap, and roughly dice the horns of plenty and chanterelles. Lightly sauté these mushrooms in the remaining butter. Add the enoki to the other mushrooms and cook for a further minute. Set aside.

Cook the turnip in boiling salted water until tender; drain and blend it with a little water to obtain a thick, creamy purée.

To serve, place the sliced chestnuts and pomegranate seeds on the chestnut purée 'carpet' on each plate. Add the mushrooms. Dress the plates with drops of chervil oil and the sweet potato and turnip purées. Finish with purple shiso leaves, aniseed-flavoured herbs like fennel or tarragon or micro herbs.

• • •

Sardine Empanada

I love sardines – fried, marinated, roasted or barbecued, with rice or even as empanadas. The charm of this empanada is that it protects the sardines' tender flesh from direct contact with the heat and adds a crusty texture without masking the natural taste of the fish. It's a type of 'crostino' that could easily be adapted to other recipes.

Serves 4

1 frozen pre-baked loaf of white bread
16 fresh sardines, filleted
150g ripe tomatoes
50g diced courgette
50g diced aubergine
100ml olive oil
75g diced onion
75g diced green pepper
75g diced red pepper
chervil oil
sea salt and freshly ground black
    pepper
chervil leaves, to garnish

Cut the crusts off the loaf of bread. Using a slicing machine (or a very sharp bread knife), slice the frozen bread into the thinnest possible slices. You need 32 slices. Set aside to thaw.

Next make the brine by dissolving 10g salt in 100ml warm water; cool. Add the sardine fillets to the brine and leave for 10 minutes to remove traces of blood and to season them. Drain and dry on kitchen paper, then set aside.

Blanch (14 seconds), peel, seed and dice the tomatoes. Sprinkle some sea salt over the courgette and aubergine and leave them to drain; this will remove any bitterness.

Heat a little of the olive oil in a pan and fry the onion for 5 minutes over a moderate flame. Add the peppers and continue frying for 3 minutes, then add the courgette and aubergine and cook for a further 4 minutes. Stir in the tomatoes and stew them until softened. Check the seasoning. Remove from the heat and keep warm.

Trim each slice of bread so it is slightly larger than a sardine fillet. Lay a fillet on top of each slice. Heat a little olive oil in a frying pan. A few at a time, put the slices of bread, with the sardines on top, in the pan and cook over a gentle heat until the bread is toasted golden brown and the sardine is cooked too (the bread will transfer the heat to the sardine – do not turn over). As each batch is cooked, keep hot.

To serve, spoon the cooked vegetable mixture on to the plates and lay the sardine empanadas, bread side down, on top. Season with chervil oil and garnish with chervil leaves.

• • •

Vanilla Cream with Apricot Coulis

Somewhere between a custard and a flan, this vanilla cream is baked in the oven at a lower temperature than cooks would normally do. Controlled low-temperature cooking is a technique used more and more because it respects the intrinsic flavours of the raw materials and helps to create new textures. This dessert is somewhat like a crème brûlée, but instead of cream and caramel we opt for a refreshing apricot coulis.

Serves 8

375ml whipping cream
125ml full cream milk
1 teaspoon cornflour, mixed with a little milk to dissolve
2 vanilla pods, split in half
1 egg
6 egg yolks
150g caster sugar, plus extra for caramelising
lemon verbena leaves, to decorate

For the apricot coulis
6–8 apricots
100g caster sugar

Preheat the oven to 100°C (conventional oven 120°C/Gas Mark ½).

Heat the cream and milk with the halved vanilla pods in a saucepan. Remove from the heat just before boiling point. Whisk in the cornflour until the mix is lightly thickened. Scrape the vanilla seeds into the hot liquid, then discard the pods. Leave to cool slightly.

Whisk together the egg, egg yolks and sugar until creamy. Pour in the warm vanilla cream and stir to mix. Divide among eight ramekins or similar containers.

Set the ramekins in a bain marie or roasting tin containing hot water and bake for about 45 minutes until just set. To test if the custards are ready, prick them with a knife; it should come out clean. Lift the ramekins out of the water and cool, then chill for at least 12 hours.

To make the coulis, dice the apricots, then combine with the sugar and 100ml water in a saucepan. Cook gently for 10 minutes until the apricots are very soft. Leave to cool, then chill. (If you prefer a smooth coulis, purée the fruit and syrup.)

To serve, turn out a vanilla cream on to each rounded plate. Sprinkle the surface of the cream with sugar and caramelise it with a kitchen blowtorch. Alternatively, leave the cream in the ramekins and sprinkle the surface with sugar before placing under the grill to caramelise. Add the apricot coulis and decorate with lemon verbena leaves.

● ● ●

Ruth
Rogers

'Less is more.'

Rogers

hanks to its riverside position, the multi-award-winning River Café in London's Hammersmith district is often referred to as a little piece of Italy on the Thames. That accolade is due entirely to its founders – self-taught chef and restaurateur Ruth Rogers and her business and culinary partner, the late, much missed Rose Gray.

They launched the River Café in 1987 and by doing so not only created a much loved and admired restaurant but also inspired a generation of British chefs: most famously Jamie Oliver, who went on to found his own restaurant empire and conquer culinary television worldwide.

Indeed, her contribution to the restaurant world was recognised when Rogers received an MBE (Member of the British Empire) award from Queen Elizabeth II in 2010. It was a very long way from making pasta (with Gray on sandwich duties) when the River Café was launched.

American-born Rogers came to London in 1967 to study graphic design and never left. A keen home cook with no formal training, she and Gray opened their iconic restaurant next to the offices of Rogers' architect husband Richard (now Lord) Rogers, ostensibly to feed his staff who had nowhere to eat at the time. They never looked back.

Rogers' initial interest in cooking was ignited by her Italian mother-in-law, Dada, and by trips to Italy. Time spent in France, while her husband was designing the Pompidou Centre, Paris, reinforced her growing belief in the importance of seasonal cooking and well-sourced produce: something on which she has never, ever compromised.

When she first started her culinary career, Rogers' commitment to artisan-produced, regional Italian produce,

presented simply in a relaxed dining room, clashed with the fine-dining fashion of the day. But numerous awards (including a coveted Michelin star in 1988), coupled with wider recognition on television and millions of cookbooks sold, proved that Rogers was merely ahead of her time.

Not surprisingly the simplicity and flavours of the River Café cuisine spill into Rogers' own home where the kitchen serves as the meeting space for her family of five children and 12 grandchildren. It's here she prepares favourite pasta dishes, or the zabaglione ice cream recipe handed down to her from her mother-in-law, 'a brilliant Italian cook'.

• • •

Secret Food Haunt

La Fromagerie, a London cheesemonger specialising in artisan cheeses sourced from the UK, USA and Europe. It has a reputation as the best supplier of Italian regional cheeses in the city and has two shops and maturing cellars, plus a café, No 6 La Fromagerie. It also sells fine European charcuterie, wines, bread, home-made jams and chutneys, fresh fruit and vegetables.

Vignole of Braised Artichokes, Peas, Broad Beans with Prosciutto

A Roman dish celebrating the time when artichokes, peas and broad beans are in season.

Serves 4

500g podded fresh broad beans
500g podded fresh peas
4 globe artichokes
about 3 tablespoons extra virgin
    olive oil
200g fresh new springtime onions,
    peeled and sliced
10 prosciutto slices
3 tablespoons chopped mint
sea salt and freshly ground black
    pepper

Separate the large broad beans from the small ones. Do the same with the peas.

To prepare the artichokes, pull away the tough outer leaves, trim the stalks and cut off the tough tips. Trim the artichokes down to the hearts and tender, pale green leaves. Cut each artichoke lengthways in half and then into quarters. Cut away any choke.

Heat the olive oil in a thick-bottomed saucepan. Add the onions and cook briefly to soften, then add the artichokes. Fry together for 5 minutes, lightly colouring the vegetables. Add the larger broad beans and peas and continue to fry, stirring to coat all the vegetables with oil, for another 5 minutes.

Add the remaining peas and broad beans and stir to mix. Pour in 100ml of hot water, just to cover the vegetables, then lay four or five slices of prosciutto over the surface. Cover the pan and simmer gently for about 30 minutes until all the vegetables are tender. If the liquid dries out, add more olive oil, not water.

Season and stir in the chopped mint. Serve with the remaining prosciutto and pieces of bruschetta.

• • •

Gallo Cedrone con Fegato
(Roast Grouse with Liver Crostino)

*Grouse is my favourite game bird. The addition of Chianti 'Italianates' the
classic British way of cooking grouse. Twenty minutes of roasting will give
you a grouse that is on the rare side; 25 minutes will give you medium –
that is, the legs cooked, lightly pink near the breast. A blue grouse will take
no more than a total of 15 minutes to roast.*

Serves 2

2 grouse, wiped clean, with their livers
   and hearts intact inside, if possible
2 sprigs of sage
2 sprigs of thyme
70g unsalted butter
150ml Italian brandy
1 bottle of Chianti Classico Reserva
2 slices of sourdough bread
1 garlic clove, peeled
sea salt and freshly ground black
   pepper

Preheat the oven to 200°C (conventional oven 220°C/Gas Mark 6). Season the
cavity of each grouse with salt and pepper. Put half the herbs inside each grouse
with a knob of the butter. Wipe the birds all over with the brandy and season the
skin with sea salt.

Heat 30g of the butter in an ovenproof pan or flameproof casserole that will
hold the birds snugly. When the butter is hot, add the grouse and lightly brown
on all sides, finishing with them breast side up. Add 15g butter to the pan, then
transfer to the oven to roast for 10 minutes.

Add a glass of the Chianti and roast for a further 10 minutes (or longer
if you want the grouse cooked medium). Remove the grouse from the pan
and place them in a warm bowl. Spoon out the livers and hearts, if they are
there, and chop them.

Add the rest of the brandy, another 15g butter and another glass of wine to
the pan juices. Over a high heat, boil for about 5 minutes until reduced to a
thick, glossy sauce.

Grill or toast the bread on each side. Rub one side only with the garlic clove.
Dip the garlicky side of each crostino into the sauce and place this side up on
heated plates. Spread the chopped livers and hearts over the crostino.

Add the juices from the bowl the grouse have been resting in to the sauce, then
set a bird on top of each crostino. Pour over the remaining sauce. Serve with
watercress or rocket dressed with olive oil and lemon juice, and drink the rest
of the Chianti.

• • •

Blood Orange Sorbet

A winter sorbet and a divine way to finish a rich meal.
This should be served on the same day as it is made.

Serves 10

15 blood oranges, unwaxed if possible
caster sugar
2 unwaxed lemons

Juice all but one of the oranges and measure the volume of liquid. Use half that volume of caster sugar.

Cut the lemons and the remaining orange into quarters and remove the pips. Place in a food processor or blender with the sugar and pulse-chop to a liquid. Add the orange juice and pulse once or twice to mix.

Pour into an ice cream machine and churn until frozen. The sorbet can be transferred to a suitable container and kept in the freezer for a couple of hours before serving.

• • •

Curtis
Stone

'A sharp, high quality knife is hands-down the most important tool you can have in the kitchen.'

Stone

Best known to his many fans in the USA and Australia as a television chef and personality, Curtis Stone nevertheless owes his current starry status to years working in top-class London restaurants. He's recently fulfilled a lifelong dream by opening his first solo restaurant, Maude (named after his grandmother), in Los Angeles – a venture that places him firmly back in the kitchen.

The name is fitting, as the Melbourne-born Stone learned to cook fudge at his grandmother's apron strings at the age of four. However, despite this early encouragement, he gained a business degree before the call of the kitchen won out. Initial culinary training in Australia was followed by eight years in London working for his culinary hero, the legendary British chef Marco Pierre White, at the latter's renowned fine-dining eateries.

Chiselled good looks and a charismatic Aussie personality meant Stone soon ventured out of the kitchen on to television: first in the UK, then Australia and America. These days, having moved to Los Angeles in 2006, he hosts many top-rated US cookery shows, including Food Network's *All-Star Academy,* and he regularly co-hosts CBS' award-winning cooking and talk show *The Rachael Ray Show*.

At the moment, Maude keeps him busy (the restaurant has already won a string of awards from Los Angeles and national publications, including being named one of the Best New Restaurants in the world in 2015 by *Travel + Leisure* magazine, and the city's Best New Restaurant for 2014 by *LA Weekly*) but weekends, if free, are a time 'to just hang out' with his wife, actress Lindsay Price, and their two children. That might involve hitting Malibu beach for a surf, a dip in the pool, or trying out new recipes he's been 'eyeing up' in magazines or books.

Secret Food Haunt

The Oaks Gourmet in Los Angeles, a quality-driven neighbourhood market/deli/café on North Bronson Avenue, which sells everything from craft beers to artisan cheeses and chocolates. Sandwiches, pizzas and breakfasts feature heavily on the menu. 'The brekky burrito is pretty insane, especially slathered in hot sauce'.

Stone doesn't do restaurant food at home, preferring a more casual approach and long, lazy meals. 'I love cooking any brunch dish – we let brunch carry on for hours.' Don't bet against seeing crumpets and crêpes topped with seasonal fruits, spreads or syrups on Stone's home table, nor against being served Brussels sprouts, a very undervalued ingredient in his opinion, which Stone serves 'every which way – except mushy and bland!'

• • •

Thyme and Fennel-crusted Pork Roast
with Calvados Apple Compote

One of my favourite family meals growing up was my mum's and granny's roast pork. No matter where I am, just smelling pork as it roasts brings back wonderful childhood memories. A joint with the skin on is what you want, the skin turns into a delicious crunchy crackling – my favourite part – while the fat beneath it bastes the pork naturally as it roasts and lends great flavour. I like to brine the pork loin for more flavour and added juiciness, but if you don't have the time, you can skip the brine. The pork will still be super tasty.

Serves 6

1 x 1.5–1.8kg bone-in pork loin (with
  skin still intact)
1 tablespoon sea salt
3 garlic cloves, peeled
1 tablespoon fennel seeds
2 tablespoons thyme leaves
1 teaspoon freshly ground black pepper
2 tablespoons olive oil

For the brine

150g sea salt
100g sugar
1 head garlic, halved horizontally and
  cloves separated
1 tablespoon black peppercorns

For the apple compote

700g Fuji apples (about 3 large),
  peeled, cored and each cut
  into 8 wedges
2 whole cloves
180ml Calvados
about 1 tablespoon caster sugar

To prepare the brine, put the salt and sugar in a large pot with 750ml of water. Stir over medium–high heat for about 5 minutes until the salt and sugar dissolve. Stir in the garlic and peppercorns, then set aside for 10 minutes to allow the flavours to infuse the seasoned water. Stir in a further 1.5 litres water. Leave the brine to cool completely.

Using a sharp knife or a box cutter, score the skin and fat that covers the top of the pork. Place the pork loin in the brine so that only the pork meat is submerged but the skin remains above the brine. Refrigerate, uncovered, for at least 12 hours.

Remove the pork from the brine and pat it dry with kitchen paper (discard the brine). Line a baking tray with dry kitchen paper and set the pork, bone side down, on the tray. Refrigerate, uncovered, for about 1 hour to allow the pork to dry a bit.

Preheat the oven to 230°C (conventional oven 250°C/Gas Mark 10), and position a rack on the lowest rung of the oven. While it is heating, transfer the pork, bone side down, to a rack in a heavy roasting tin and leave at room temperature for 30 minutes to take off some of the chill.

In a mortar and pestle, grind the salt with the garlic cloves to form a paste. Add the fennel seeds and grind to break them up. Add the thyme leaves and grind them into the salt mixture. Mix in the pepper and oil. Rub the thyme mixture all over the pork and into the scored surface.

Roast the pork for 30 minutes, or until the skin blisters and becomes crisp and golden brown, then turn the oven down to 175°C (conventional oven 195°C/Gas Mark 4) and continue roasting for about 45 minutes; the pork is done when an instant-read meat thermometer inserted into the centre of the joint registers 60°C. Remove the tin from the oven and allow the pork to rest for 30 minutes before carving.

Meanwhile, make the apple compote. In a heavy large saucepan, stir the apples with the cloves over medium–high heat for about 5 minutes until the apples just begin to soften and caramelise slightly. Turn the heat down to medium–low, add the Calvados and cook, stirring, for about 5 minutes until the liquid has reduced by half. Cover the pan and continue cooking the apples, stirring occasionally, for about 8 minutes until they are tender and most of the juices have evaporated. Remove the pan from the heat.

Using a potato masher, coarsely mash the apples. Stir in enough sugar to sweeten the compote slightly (this can be made a day ahead and kept in the fridge; warm it gently in a covered pan before serving).

Thinly slice the pork on a carving board and arrange the slices on plates. Drizzle over any juices exuded from the pork during carving. Spoon the apple compote alongside the pork and serve.

• • •

Ricotta Pancakes with Melted Raspberries and Sweet Lemon Butter

I perfected these pancakes as a young chef while working at The Savoy Hotel in Melbourne, and have been making them ever since. Truly, they are my all-time favourite pancakes! Now that my son Hudson is walking and talking, I like to make big pancakes for the grown-ups and fifty-cent-sized pancakes for him. I call the raspberries 'melted' because they're quickly cooked with a touch of sugar just until they begin to soften and release their juice, but still retain their beautiful shape. Beating icing sugar and lemon zest into the butter makes it creamy and lighter in texture (not to mention utterly delicious!) – perfect for spreading over these pancakes, or waffles, toast, crumpets or scones. A good morning, indeed.

Serves 4

For the sweet lemon butter
115g unsalted butter, softened
30g icing sugar, sifted
2 teaspoons fresh lemon juice
1 teaspoon finely grated lemon zest

For the melted raspberries
340g fresh raspberries
50g caster sugar
2 teaspoons finely grated lemon zest

For the pancakes
250g fresh ricotta cheese
4 medium eggs, separated
180ml buttermilk
125g plain flour
1½ teaspoons baking powder
a pinch of salt
50g caster sugar
about 45g unsalted butter

First make the sweet lemon butter. Combine the ingredients in a medium bowl and beat with an electric mixer until smooth and creamy. Set aside at room temperature.

To make the melted raspberries, heat a large, heavy frying pan over medium–high heat. Add the raspberries, sugar and lemon zest and cook for about 45 seconds until the sugar melts and the berries soften only slightly and begin to release their juice to form a syrup. Don't let the berries cook too long or they will become mushy and lose their beautiful shape. Remove from the heat and keep warm.

To make the pancakes, whisk together the ricotta and egg yolks in a large bowl to blend, then whisk in the buttermilk. Sift the flour, baking powder and salt into the ricotta mixture and whisk once more until just combined.

In a separate bowl, whisk the egg whites with the sugar just until stiff peaks form. Using a large silicone spatula, gently fold the egg whites through the batter in two batches.

Heat a flat, smooth griddle pan over medium–low heat. Melt some of the unsalted butter on the griddle. Make the pancakes in batches of about three at a time (or more if you are making small pancakes). Ladle the batter on to the griddle and cook the pancakes for about 3 minutes per side until they puff, turn golden brown and are just cooked through. Transfer the pancakes to plates.

Immediately after the pancakes come off the griddle, spread some sweet lemon butter over them and spoon on some of the warm melted raspberries and the accumulated raspberry syrup, then serve. Repeat to make and serve more pancakes.

• • •

Chocolate Mousse Soufflés with Peppermint Ganache and Whipped Crème Fraîche

After making many different soufflés throughout my career, this gem won me over with its warm chocolate mousse-like texture and impressive rising soufflé power. Who could resist its fluffy yet creamy texture and deep chocolatey goodness? Not me! I love the refreshing flavour of mint – it's one of my go-to ingredients in sweet and savoury dishes. Here, it works like a dream in this classic pairing with chocolate. And this soufflé just happens to be gluten-free, something I never set out to achieve when I created it many moons ago, but which has become an added bonus today.

Serves 6

For the soufflés
15g unsalted butter, softened
105g caster sugar
115g high-quality dark chocolate
    (65–70% cocoa solids), chopped
30g cocoa powder
6 medium egg whites
icing sugar, for dusting (optional)

For the peppermint ganache and whipped crème fraîche
310ml whipping cream
115g high-quality dark chocolate
    (65–70% cocoa solids), chopped
¼ teaspoon pure peppermint extract
60ml crème fraîche, stirred to blend

Preheat the oven to 175°C (conventional oven to 195°C/Gas Mark 4). Coat the interiors of six 225ml soufflé dishes completely with the butter, then coat with 45g of the caster sugar. Place the dishes on a heavy baking tray.

Set a large heatproof bowl over a saucepan of simmering water. Add the chocolate and stir until melted and smooth. Whisk in the cocoa powder and 125ml cold water until smooth. Remove from the heat and set aside.

In another large bowl, whisk the egg whites until foamy. Gradually whisk in the remaining caster sugar. Continue whisking until the egg whites are glossy and will form soft peaks when the whisk is removed.

Fold a quarter of the egg whites into the warm chocolate mixture to lighten it, then fold in the remaining whites (the mixture will resemble chocolate mousse). Immediately divide the soufflé mixture equally among the prepared soufflé dishes. Set aside at room temperature while you prepare the ganache and whipped crème fraîche.

To make the ganache, heat 180ml of the whipping cream in a small heavy saucepan over medium–high heat just until hot. Remove the pan from the heat, add the chocolate and cover. Set aside for 5 minutes, then add the peppermint extract and whisk just until blended.

Meanwhile, whisk the remaining whipping cream in a large bowl until thick and fluffy. Fold in the crème fraîche.

Bake the soufflés for about 10 minutes until they rise but are still moist and creamy in the centre. Dust the soufflés with powdered sugar at the table and serve the ganache and whipped crème fraîche alongside so your guests can spoon as much ganache and crème over their dessert as they please.

• • •

David
Thompson

'I was sacked from my first cooking job. I had my mother's talent then.'

Thompson

I t is no exaggeration to say that Sydney-born chef and writer David Thompson is revered as one of the world's experts in Thai cuisine. From royal Thai cuisine to Thai street food, his knowledge is unsurpassed. He wasn't, though, imbued with a love of food – of any sort, let alone Thai – during his childhood, when early culinary influences can only be described as meagre ('my mother was the world's worst cook!').

Instead, Thompson's culinary epiphany came when he visited Bangkok in 1986, a city in which he has lived on-and-off ever since, and was seduced by the country and, particularly, its food. Hooked by the diversity of ingredients, and the depth and balance of tastes on offer, he stayed in the city for three years, immersing himself in Thailand's remarkable cuisine.

Having found his forte, Thompson returned to Australia in 1992 and opened the Darley Street Thai in Sydney. His culinary flair and fanatical attention to high-quality Thai ingredients soon earned him an enviable reputation and garnered numerous awards, as well as a second Sydney restaurant and an offer to open a Thai restaurant at Christina Ong's Halkin hotel in London.

And so Nahm was born in 2001. It received immediate critical acclaim, gaining a highly sought-after Michelin star within six months – the first Thai restaurant to do so. A Nahm in Bangkok opened at that city's Metropolitan hotel in 2010 – it was named Best Restaurant in Asia in 2014 by San Pellegrino's highly regarded Asia's Top 50 Best Restaurants list.

Having closed the London restaurant because of increasing European regulations about importing Thai ingredients, Thompson now lives, once again, in Bangkok. An inveterate traveller (he spent three months in the Amazon in 2014), he has an insatiable quest for learning about food and rarely has time off. 'I have absolutely no idea what a weekend is. It's a chef's lot.'

When he does cook for friends he'll often choose a 'riveting jungle curry – spicy, aromatic, dangerous and delicious', and has a very Thai penchant for fermented food, kanom jin noodles being a case in point. 'They're slightly fermented rice noodles, delicious when eaten with sauces made with chicken and wild ginger, or with a myriad of fresh Thai herbs dressed with coconut cream, or one of those pungent jungle curries.'

• • •

Secret Food Haunt
Bangkok's wet markets, such Khlong Toei market. Found on the canal systems of the city, 'real and unreformed', they sell everything from spices and herbs – including curry pastes – to vegetables, meat and street food.

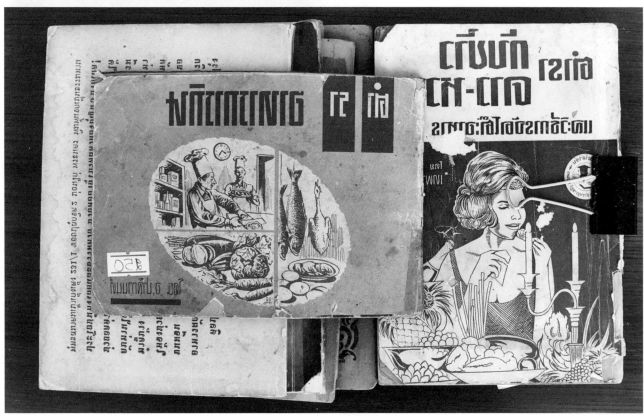

Grilled Omelette
(Kai Bpam)

Thai food doesn't have to be complicated and these eggs are a splendid
example of it. All you need are good eggs, good fish sauce and a fire
(though a cast iron pan will do).

**Serves 2 (with steamed rice)
or 3 (with rice and the other
dishes on pages 306 and 309)**

100g fresh banana leaves
4 eggs
2 tablespoons fish sauce
a pinch of white pepper
1 tablespoon chopped spring
onions

First make a banana leaf boat. To do this you'll need two pieces of cleaned banana leaf, one about 30 x 25cm and the other slightly smaller. Use the larger piece as the base, placing it so the darker side is facing down. Place the smaller piece on top with its darker side facing up. Now fold up one short end; gather and fold its corners together while curving up the long sides of the boat, then secure with a wooden toothpick. Do the same with the other short end.

Should you not have a banana tree handy, then you can use a small cast iron pan instead.

Combine the eggs with the fish sauce, pepper and spring onions. Pour into the prepared banana leaf boat and grill over hot charcoal (or cook in an extremely hot cast iron pan for 3–4 minutes) until the omelette is just set and the bottom is slightly charred.

Allow to cool somewhat before serving.

• • •

Mixed Vegetable and Fruit Salad dressed with Tamarind, Palm Sugar and Sesame Seeds (Yam Pak)

While not every suggested vegetable is necessary, a good selection gives a rounded balance to the salad.

Serves 2 (with rice) or 3 (with rice and the other dishes on pages 305 and 309)

A mixture of some or all of the following
a handful of mixed herbs, e.g. mint leaves, dill sprigs and Thai, holy and lemon basil
30g sliced yam bean/jicama
2 tablespoons sliced green beans
1 tablespoon shredded pak chi farang/ long-leaf coriander
flesh from ½ small green mango, shredded
2 lemongrass stalks, trimmed and finely sliced
1 apple aubergine, sliced
4 kaffir limes leaves, shredded
½ star fruit/carambola, elegantly sliced
2 red shallots, thickly sliced

For the dressing
70g dried tamarind pulp
2 tablespoons light soy sauce (the Thai brand Som Bun is the one I use)
200g palm sugar
2 tablespoons toasted sesame seeds
2 tablespoons deep-fried shallots

To garnish
3 deep-fried large, dried red chillies, coarsely crushed

To make the dressing, soak the tamarind pulp in 60ml water for a few minutes to soften, then squeeze and work the pulp to dissolve it. Strain the liquid (discard the fibres and seeds in the sieve). Put the resulting tamarind water and light soy sauce in a bowl, add the palm sugar and stir to dissolve. Toast the sesame seeds in a dry pan until fragrant and golden; allow to cool. Crush the sesame seeds with the deep-fried shallots in a pestle and mortar, then stir into the tamarind mixture. The dressing should taste sweet, sour and only very slightly salty. It might be necessary to lighten with a few tablespoons of water.

Combine the prepared fruits and vegetables in a bowl. Toss with all the dressing (this is quite a wet dish) and serve, sprinkled with the crushed deep-fried chillies.

• • •

Jungle Curry of Salted Beef with Thai Basil and Green Peppercorns (Geng Bpaa bai Madan Neua Kem)

Madan leaves are sour, like sorrel.

Serves 2 (with steamed rice) or 3 (with rice and the other dishes on pages 305 and 306)

For the grilled salted beef (neua kem yang)
100g boneless beef, ideally flank, rump cap or rib lip
1 tablespoon fish sauce
a pinch of salt
a pinch of caster sugar
a pinch of white pepper

For the red jungle paste
12 dried, long red chillies, seeded and soaked in water until soft, then squeezed dry
1 fresh, long red chilli – no need to remove seeds
a pinch of salt
a few Thai bird's eye chillies/'scuds'
1 stalk lemongrass
8 slices galangal, peeled
1 small piece kaffir lime zest, any bitter white pith removed
2 stalks grachai/wild ginger
2 red shallots, peeled
3 garlic cloves, peeled
1 coriander root, cleaned
½ teaspoon gapi/Thai shrimp paste

For the garlic paste
1 garlic clove, peeled
2 Thai bird's eye chillies/'scuds'
1g sea salt
a pinch of Thai basil buds

For the curry
2 tablespoons lard or vegetable oil
250ml chicken stock or water
2–3 kaffir lime leaves, torn
2 heaped tablespoons red jungle paste (see above)
1 teaspoon fish sauce
a pinch of caster sugar

1 cup madan leaves, shredded, or 2 tablespoons tamarind water or lime juice
3 large green chillies (20g), sliced lengthways
2 Thai bird's eye chillies/'scuds'
2 stalks grachai/wild ginger (10g), peeled and shredded
5 stalks fresh green peppercorns (20g)
1½ teaspoons fish sauce (10g)
a handful of Thai basil leaves (5g) (optional)

For the salted beef, cut the meat, along the grain, into long slices about 5mm thick (chilling it first will make slicing easier). Work the fish sauce, salt, sugar and pepper into the beef, then cover and set aside to marinate in the fridge for a few hours.

Lay the beef strips on a rack in a warm, airy place. Make sure the strips are sufficiently spaced so air can circulate around them. Leave to dry, turning them over at least once, for about 24 hours until quite firm and almost dried. If you have a food dehydrator, use it to dry the beef

Grill the beef, ideally over charcoal, turning several times, until thoroughly cooked and smoky. Bruise the beef with a pestle and mortar – this opens up the meat and softens the fibres. When somewhat cool, tear the beef along the grain into bite-sized pieces.

To make the red jungle paste, pound the ingredients, adding them one at a time in the order given, in the mortar and pestle to achieve quite a smooth paste. (If there is any paste left over it can be kept in the fridge for a week).

For the garlic paste, pound the ingredients together to make a somewhat coarse paste.

Now make the curry. Heat the lard or oil in a shallow pan or sauteuse (sauté pan) and fry the garlic paste until light golden. Moisten with the stock, then add the kaffir lime leaves and stir in the jungle paste. Simmer for a moment.

Add the beef and continue to simmer for a minute. Stir in the fish sauce and sugar and simmer for another minute or so.

Add the shredded madan leaves, large green chillies and scuds, grachai and green peppercorns. Season once again with fish sauce to taste. The curry should taste slightly salty, spicy and sour. Finish with Thai basil leaves. The curry will improve if it sits for several minutes before serving. Serve with jasmin rice.

• • •

T

Mitch
Tonks

'I love avocado on bread and toast instead of butter.'

Tonks

Appropriately enough for one of the UK's most passionate seafood champions, you'll often find restaurateur and self-taught chef Mitch Tonks out on the water at the weekend. 'An early start for a day's sail with some food aboard, and to stay somewhere at anchor for the night, is my ideal day.'

Tonks acquired his love of the sea during formative years sailing and fishing as a boy in his hometown of Weston-super-Mare in the west of England. His love for fish and seafood grew naturally and one of his treasured childhood memories is peeling brown shrimps with his mother and grandmother for 'the sweetest sandwich[es] ever' on Friday afternoons. (Unsurprisingly, he's passed this passion for the produce of the sea on to his own son, Dominic – one of his five children – who is also a fishmonger).

Despite this, Tonks trained for a career as an accountant. However, by the age of 27 he had swapped his ledgers for an apron and opened his first specialist fishmongers, FishWorks, in Bath.

Not content with just selling fish, Tonks taught himself to cook through the books of legendary British food writers Elizabeth David and Jane Grigson, although by his own admission he's never managed to conquer making desserts. In the meantime, his FishWorks business grew steadily into an award-winning chain of 13 restaurants and fishmongers, including a top-end wholesale fish business supplying the country's leading hotels.

Books, television appearances and numerous awards and accolades soon followed (including a World Gourmand Cookbook award for his book *Fresh*), as he became one of the country's most high-profile seafood chefs and a leading campaigner for sustainable fishing.

At the same time Tonks lessened his involvement in –

and eventually parted company with – FishWorks. But restauranteuring was in his blood, and with Mat Prowse he opened The Seahorse in Dartmouth in 2007. It soon won Best UK Restaurant in the *Observer Food Magazine* Awards and Best Fish Restaurant in the UK's influential *Good Food Guide*.

Most recently, he's opened a string of fish and chip restaurants and grills across the West Country. But that's no surprise for someone who likes nothing better than sneaking crabsticks doused in vinegar from his local seafood shack.

• • •

> ### Secret Food Haunt
> C. M. McCabe, an 'old school' butcher in Totnes, Devon. Sausages, home-cured bacon and, naturally, pasties are specialities. 'The meat is fabulous. He isn't cheffy or trendy – he's a proper shopkeeper.'

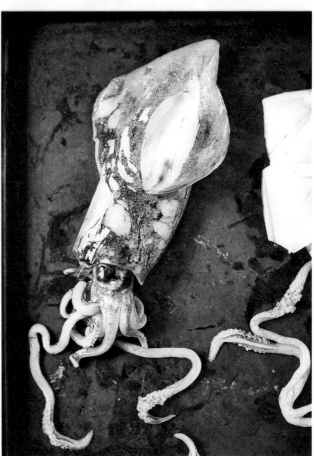

Calamari in Umido

For this dish we use the very small baby squid at the start of their season. They are so tender and sweet, and perfect cooked this way as they almost melt when you eat them. If no small squid are available larger can be used but the bodies are best split open and scored with a sharp knife – on the diagonal first one way then the other so as to produce a diamond pattern – then cut into small strips so that when they cook they roll up into small tubes.

Serves 2

6 small squid, about 100g each, skinned and cleaned (with tentacles)
100ml olive oil
2 garlic cloves, finely sliced on a mandoline
½ dried bird's eye chilli
10 cherry tomatoes (preferably Datterini), peeled
1 tablespoon shredded flat-leaf parsley
½ lemon
salt

Rinse the squid thoroughly and dry on kitchen paper.

Heat the olive oil in a frying pan with a little salt, add the sliced garlic and chilli, and fry gently for a few minutes until the edges of the garlic just start to take on a golden colour.

Add the whole small squid with their tentacles and the peeled tomatoes and continue cooking, gently squeezing the tomatoes with a fork so as to release some of their juices. After 2–3 minutes the squid will have turned from translucent to pure white and a lovely emulsion will have formed from the oil and tomato juices.

Remove from the heat. Add the parsley and a good squeeze of lemon and season with salt to taste. Stir well, then serve immediately.

● ● ●

Lobster Caldereta

I first came across this dish on the island of Menorca where many versions of the Caldereta are served. The lobster there has such a wonderful flavour and the long cooking allows the shell to release its flavour into the broth. It really is a delight. The Caldereta is the clay pot it is cooked in, so use a nice clay or well-seasoned casserole dish to cook and serve from.

Serves 2

1 live lobster, about 750g
olive oil
25ml Spanish brandy
1 red pepper, roasted, peeled and seeded
4 very ripe tomatoes, skinned and seeded
2 garlic cloves, finely chopped
1 dried bird's eye chilli, crumbled
1 sprig of thyme
a few saffron threads
a handful of parsley, chopped
salt and freshly ground black pepper

For the sauce
2 garlic cloves, crushed to a paste
4 salted anchovy fillets, rinsed
olive oil
50ml white wine
1 teaspoon dried oregano
2g saffron threads
1 litre good shellfish stock (made from roasted shellfish shells)
400ml tomato passata, preferably freshly made

For the salt dough
200g rock salt
200g plain flour

First subdue the lobster by chilling it well in the freezer for 2 hours before you need it. Place it on a chopping board, and lay a tea towel over the tail and hold the tail down. Insert a large cook's knife down through the cross on the back of the lobster's head. The nerve centre lies below this cross, so the lobster will be killed instantly. Chop the lobster into pieces in the shell. Discard the pouch that lies close to the head.

Next, make the sauce. Gently fry the garlic and anchovies in a little olive oil for a minute or so, then add the wine and boil to reduce by half. Add the oregano and saffron. Pour in the stock and passata, and season with salt and pepper. Bring to a simmer, then move to the back of the stove and leave to tick over on a low heat for 2–3 hours, to reduce slightly and develop a deep flavour.

Now you can make the Caldereta. Preheat the oven to 140°C (conventional oven 160°F/Gas Mark 3). Heat a good splash of olive oil in a flameproof casserole and roast the lobster pieces until the shell turns red all over. Add the brandy and boil until it has almost all evaporated, then add the red pepper, tomatoes, garlic, chilli, thyme and saffron. Cover with about half of the sauce (the remainder can be saved to make another Caldereta.)

To make the salt dough, mix the salt and flour with enough cold water to bind together to a dough. Put the lid on the casserole and seal the join with the salt dough. Place in the oven and cook for 1 hour. Before serving, check the seasoning and stir in the chopped parsley.

• • •

Espresso Panna Cotta

This dessert is a firm favourite after dinner at The Seahorse. We serve it in little coffee cups and recommend a brandy or two with it! It's really easy to make and is a great party dessert.

Serves 12

4 gelatine leaves
220ml espresso coffee
220ml milk
120ml caster sugar
100ml brandy
360ml double cream

For the syrup
300ml caster sugar
125ml espresso coffee
25ml brandy

Soften the gelatine leaves in water as per the packet instructions. Gently heat the espresso with the milk and sugar in a saucepan, stirring to help dissolve the sugar. Squeeze excess water out of the gelatine, then add to the pan and stir until completely melted. Remove the pan from the heat and add the brandy. Leave the mixture to cool.

Whip the cream until it is in soft peaks. Gently fold into the coffee mixture, keeping as much of the whisked-in air as possible. Divide the mixture among espresso coffee cups or other small moulds and chill in the fridge to set.

Make the syrup by warming the sugar in a pan until melted, then let it bubble away until it has become a sticky caramel (take care not to let it get too dark and burn). Add the coffee and brandy and stir until smoothly combined. Leave to cool.

Serve the panna cotta with the syrup drizzled on the top (like the crema on an espresso).

• • •

Tetsuya
Wakuda

'My most used cookbook is *The Roux Brothers on Patisserie.*'

Wakuda

Japanese-born chef Tetsuya Wakuda is one of Australia's – and Asia's – culinary giants. His unique fusion of Franco-Japanese cooking, with its pure, decisive, refined flavours, has influenced many of his peers, and can be experienced most famously at his eponymous Sydney restaurant (a high temple of gastronomy in the city for more than 25 years) and also, since 2010, at his new restaurant – Waku Ghin – in Singapore.

Born in Hamamatsu, Japan, Wakuda emigrated to Australia aged 22 with a suitcase, a passion for food and his mother's chicken karaage recipe, still a favourite of his more than 40 years later (see page 325). His first job as a kitchen hand at Fishwives Seafare Restaurant in the Sydney suburb of Surry Hills came to an end when he was snapped up to be a sushi chef at one of Sydney's most iconic restaurants, Kinsela's. And it was here that Wakuda learned classical French cooking techniques, while experimenting with the flavours of fresh seasonal produce.

It didn't take him long to work out that he'd like to open his own successful restaurant in Sydney, an ambition he realised in 1989 when Tetsuya's first opened its doors at its original site in the city's Rozelle suburb (it relocated to central Sydney in 2000). It instantly earned him the highest recognition and legendary status for his signature dish: a confit of petuna ocean trout with konbu, celery and apple.

Despite the renown and elegance of his professional cuisine, Tetsuya isn't above chomping on a bit of fast food, Aussie hamburger style with all the trimmings – 'the lot, including beetroot!' He's also partial to Japanese mayonnaise, specifically the brand Kewpie.

A long-held dream is to open a restaurant in Kyoto, back in his native Japan, but Wakuda is nevertheless content living in his adopted home of Sydney, where he likes nothing better than to see what's been landed at the city's fish market. Leatherjacket, bonito or ribbonfish are favourite catches: often underrated, he believes, 'but they taste so good – deep-fried or stir-fried, or sashimi.'

• • •

Secret Food Haunt
Sydney fish market, located in the city's Blackwattle Bay two kilometres west of the Sydney CBD (central business district). The market incorporates a working fishing port, wholesale and retail fish markets, and several seafood eating outlets.

Chicken Karaage

As a child I would wait with great anticipation when my mother prepared chicken karaage. I love it so much that years ago, when we were in Rozelle, I ate karaage every day for three months. My sous chef said he would quit if I didn't stop! It was very funny.

**Serves 4 as a main dish
or 8 as a snack/finger food**

500g skinless boneless chicken thighs
1 teaspoon caster sugar
1 teaspoon salt
20g grated fresh ginger
20ml sake
25ml soy sauce
35ml mirin
1 teaspoon dark sesame oil
grapeseed oil, for deep-frying
plain flour, for dusting
cracked black pepper

Cut each chicken thigh into five or six pieces.

Mix together the sugar, salt, ginger, sake, soy sauce, mirin and sesame oil in a bowl and season with cracked black pepper. Add the pieces of chicken and mix with the seasonings. Cover with clingfilm and leave to marinate in the fridge for 30 minutes.

Heat a deep pan of grapeseed oil to 180°C. Drain off any excess marinade from the chicken pieces and lightly dust them in flour, then deep-fry (in batches) for 4–5 minutes until golden brown all over and cooked through. Drain on kitchen paper and serve hot.

• • •

Shabu Shabu Kingfish

This delicious Japanese dish is cooked and served at the table. You will need a portable tabletop burner and hotpot to cook it in, and chopsticks for all your guests. Everyone helps themselves to the ingredients and the condiments. Best flavour is achieved if the kingfish is cooked in the broth before the vegetables.

Serves 4

400g fresh kingfish fillet, thinly sliced
40g fresh wakame, rinsed
¼ head Chinese leaves, cut into small wedges
1 small leek, finely sliced
100g firm tofu (momen tofu), cut into 2cm-thick slices
6 shiitake mushrooms, cut in half
100g shimeji mushrooms
100g eringi mushrooms, quartered
100g edible chrysanthemum greens
100g sliced konnyaku

For the dipping sauce
100ml soy sauce
60ml Japanese citrus juice (di di juice)
20ml rice vinegar
2 teaspoons caster sugar

For the cooking broth
1.5 litres dashi (stock made from konbu and bonito; see cook's tips right)
1 piece dried kelp
200g daikon/mooli, finely grated

For the condiments
orange zest julienne
very finely chopped spring onion
finely grated fresh ginger
coarsely chopped salted black beans

Place the kingfish and wakame on a serving plate. Arrange the Chinese leaves, leek, tofu, mushrooms, chrysanthemum greens and konnyaku on a serving platter.

Combine the ingredients for the dipping sauce in a jug.

When you are ready to serve, prepare the cooking broth by heating the dashi to simmering point, then add the kelp. Carefully take the simmering stock to the tabletop burner and ladle or pour it into the pot. Raise the heat so the dashi simmers. Add the grated daikon, then remove the kelp.

Guests should pour a little dipping sauce into their serving bowl and flavour the sauce to their liking with the condiments.

Put the wakame into the simmering broth. Each guest should take a thin slice of kingfish, holding it with chopsticks, and literally wave the fish through the broth, then dip into the sauce and eat. The vegetables and tofu are added to the broth once all the fish has been eaten and cooked until just tender. Guests should help themselves from the pot.

The remaining cooking broth can be enjoyed at the end of the meal as is, or udon noodles can be added and cooked in the simmering broth.

Tetsuya's tip
• Freeze-dried dashi is available from Asian supermarkets to make up the required amount of stock. The mushrooms, chrysanthemum leaves and other ingredients can also be found there.

● ● ●

Braised Spatchcock
with Olives and Capers

This is another favourite recipe; it's so easy and so delicious. Also if you forget about it in the oven it still tastes great, which I did myself one Christmas. It's now a family and staff favourite.

Serves 4

2 baby chickens, about 500g each, spatchcocked and each cut in half
dry white wine
2 tablespoons salted capers, rinsed
20 black olives
4 garlic cloves, finely chopped
½ tablespoon chopped oregano
about 100ml olive oil
salt and freshly ground black pepper
1 tablespoon finely chopped fresh parsley, to garnish

Preheat the oven to 200°C (conventional oven 220°C/Gas Mark 7).

Place the spatchcock halves, skin side up, in a deep baking dish. Season with salt and pepper. Pour in enough wine until the liquid comes halfway up the sides of the spatchcocks (you can also use a mixture of wine and water). Add the capers, olives, garlic and oregano to the liquid. Drizzle the olive oil over the spatchcock halves.

Place in the oven and braise for 45 minutes until the skin is golden and spatchcocks are cooked through.

Lift each spatchcock out of the dish and place in the centre of a serving plate. Spoon over a little of the cooking liquid (including the capers and olives), garnish with chopped parsley and serve.

● ● ●

Index

Credits and Acknowledgements

Publisher Jon Croft
Commissioning Editor Meg Avent
Managing Editor Joanna Wood
Project Editor Alice Gibbs and Emily Holmes
Editor Norma MacMillan
Art Direction Matt Inwood and Kim Musgrove
Design Matt Inwood and Kim Musgrove
Design Consultant Claire Burton
Photographer David Loftus
Home Economy Elaine Byfield
Props Stylist Ange Morris
Food Stylist Genevieve Taylor and Laura Field
Assistant Food Stylist Rukmini Iyer and Laura Rowe
Proofreader Margaret Haynes
Indexer Zoe Ross

Shine would like to thank:
First and foremost, the thirty-three extraordinary chefs, thank you for your warmth and hospitality, for welcoming us into your homes and kitchens, and ultimately for sharing your favourite recipes.

To Ben Liebmann and David Loftus, for being the driving partners in bringing The Masters to life. David, thank you for your enthusiasm and dedication, and for your sense of fun...even as you were boarding yet another plane to one of the four corners of the culinary world.

To Genevieve Taylor and Laura Field for helping create and style an extraordinary collection of dishes, and to Kim Musgrove for her all-seeing and nurturing art direction and beautiful book design.

To Angela Morris, your creativity and attention to detail is found on every page, and to Claire Burton; together you helped shape and define The Masters, and ultimately kept us all on track.

To Jon Croft and Richard Charkin at Absolute and Bloomsbury for your early belief and continued support, and your patience and good humour for every change and crazy idea.

To the extraordinary team of editors, home economists, proof readers and beyond. Thank you.

And lastly, to the Shine and MasterChef family around the world. This book is a reality because of you. You have helped inspire the world in its love of food, and made MasterChef the most loved food program in the world.